OUR

NEXT

EVOLUTION

Transforming Collaborative Leadership
to Shape Our Planet's Future

LAURA CALANDRELLA

LIONCREST
PUBLISHING

OUR NEXT EVOLUTION
Transforming Collaborative Leadership to Shape Our Planet's Future

ISBN   978-1-5445-1701-8 *Hardcover*
          978-1-5445-1699-8 *Paperback*
          978-1-5445-1700-1 *Ebook*
          978-1-5445-1702-5 *Audiobook*

To past generations of leaders who have guided me toward deeper wisdom.

To future generations of leaders whose wisdom will surpass my own.

And to this beautiful planet: you will always be
the source of our greatest knowing.

CONTENTS

PREFACE

Writing a book on collaborative leadership during a global pandemic and a rising racial justice movement shook me to my core. All authors face a moment in the book writing process where they wonder, "Does my voice matter?" But what I witnessed in 2020 was all of us grappling with that same question, author or not.

In our isolation, we hungered for connection. In our division, we longed for unity. All the while, each of us tried to understand, "What is *my part* in contribution to *the whole?*"

The decade did not begin as any of us expected, yet many of us knew that there would come a day when we would have to reckon with the issues that have been lying beneath the surface for too long. Now that the day has come for this generation of leaders, we can choose to view this time with a sense of fear, or we can courageously do the work to heal the wounds of our world.

I say, choose courage.

I started writing this book during a year of deep personal transformation and growth. In the cocoon of 2019, it was born out of my conviction that the answers to our biggest questions can be found within ourselves and in relationship to one another. I still believe that's true. Though life feels more uncertain than ever, my resolve strengthens when I commit to the practices in this book and trust in their power to create change.

Does my voice matter? I wouldn't be writing this if I didn't believe it was true. I wouldn't be sharing it if I didn't believe it was true for you too. Now more than ever, we need one another to make our voices heard while celebrating their many differences. Just as important, we need to sharpen our ability to listen with curiosity and openness so that all—and I do mean *all*—voices can be heard.

My hope is that somewhere in these pages is a spark of inspiration that helps you navigate the challenges that lie ahead. Evolution is possible...for everyone.

INTRODUCTION

The first Earth Day celebration occurred in 1970 amid dire predictions that seem to echo the urgency of the crises we still face fifty years later. There was a sense of panic around the state of the planet and a guarantee that our world would change forever without immediate, decisive action.

At the time, Harvard biologist and Nobel Laureate George Wald said, "Civilization will end within fifteen to thirty years unless immediate action is taken against the problems facing mankind."[1]

Barry Commoner, a Washington University biology professor and 1980 United States presidential candidate, wrote in the scholarly journal *Environment*, "We are in an environmental crisis which threatens the survival of this nation and of the world as a suitable place of human habitation."[2]

---

[1] George Wald, "The End of Civilization Feared by Biochemist," *New York Times*, July 11, 1970, https://www.nytimes.com/1970/11/19/archives/the-end-of-civilization-feared-by-biochemist.html.

[2] "Earth Day 2008: Predictions of Environmental Disaster Were Wrong," Washington Policy Center, April 22, 2008, https://www.washingtonpolicy.org/publications/detail/earth-day-2008-predictions-of-environmental-disaster-were-wrong.

Paul Ehrlich, a Stanford biologist, was also fundamental in making predictions (and is still at work today). He shared in the vision that the path we were on was headed toward crisis. "Sometime in the next fifteen years, the end will come. And by 'the end' I mean an utter breakdown of the capacity of the planet to support humanity," he told CBS News in 1969.[3] It was this kind of energy that fueled the increase in production of food grains, a market response known as the "Green Revolution."

Of course, this was not the first time society feared environmental devastation. If we track the epistemology of conservation—that is, the theory of knowledge that distinguishes justified belief from opinion—and the way our collective understanding of what's at stake has changed over time, it's clear just how far we have come.

OUR EVOLVING CONSCIOUSNESS

A little over a century ago, a camping trip became the spark that ignited a new level of environmental consciousness in the United States. Naturalist John Muir had the full attention of President Theodore Roosevelt for three days in Yosemite Valley. Muir was a vocal and poetic advocate for protecting the natural beauty of the country, but it was Yosemite that most captured his heart. He wrote that "it was like lying in a great solemn cathedral, far vaster and more beautiful than any built by the hand of man."[4] Under the giant sequoias, a conversation unfolded between the two men that would lead Roosevelt to

---

3   Charles C. Mann, "The Book That Incited a Worldwide Fear of Overpopulation," *Smithsonian Magazine,* January 2018, https://www.smithsonianmag.com/innovation/book-incited-worldwide-fear-overpopulation-180967499/.

4   "The Camping Trip That Changed the Nation," National Parks Adventure, https://nationalparksadventure.com/the-camping-trip-that-changed-the-nation/.

protect not only Yosemite but later sign into existence five national parks, eighteen national monuments, fifty-five national bird sanctuaries and wildlife refuges, and 150 national forests.

The nation was at an inflection point in how it valued the natural world. In the East, colonization, industrialization, and urbanization decimated the forests, eroded the soil, and resulted in a rapid loss of fish and wildlife populations. The future of the American West didn't look much better. The result of Manifest Destiny was a wave of migration that was transforming wilderness into an unrecognizable landscape. This unchecked loss of resources raised alarm. The consequences were visible and impossible to ignore. A view of conservation began to emerge that included restoration, active management, and wise use of land.

Meanwhile in New England, Henry David Thoreau wandered the woods of Walden Pond. He, along with his transcendentalist friends, inspired a different sort of awareness. Through his writing, he spoke of nature as more than a commodity. He saw it as a way to transcend the boundaries set forth by society, find spiritual renewal, and "live deliberately." His words fed a generation of Americans who were hungry to celebrate their individualism. And so was born the environmental ethos of the day. By the time Teddy Roosevelt put pen to paper after his infamous camping trip, we were no longer solely driven by what we could extract from the land. We were also driven to protect it.

Our collective consciousness continued to evolve, yet always with the push-and-pull tension between managing natural resources for their use and protecting them for their intrinsic beauty. Once decimated forests became strategic assets during two world wars, heavily supporting our defenses by providing wood to build everything from airplanes to army barracks. Soon after, Aldo Leopold gently nudged the average citizen toward a holistic view of ecosystems in *A Sand County Almanac*. A land ethic took hold that he defined as "a thing is right and good when it tends to preserve the integrity, stability, and beauty of the biotic community. It is wrong when it tends otherwise."[5]

And global consciousness rose too. In 1948, the International Union for the Conservation of Nature (IUCN) brought together government and nongovernmental organizations from around the world to protect natural heritage through policy and on-the-ground initiatives.

Rachel Carson's *Silent Spring* was the precursor for a marked environmental revolution. Published in 1962, Carson wrote of a spring entirely devoid of birds singing after pesticides wreaked environmental havoc, demonstrating in a visceral way just how much was at stake. And people were listening. By connecting tactical needs to our tangible experience with nature, she was able to expose the massive health and environmental risks of unbridled use of DDT and other synthetic pesticides, leading almost directly to the formation of Earth Day, the United States Environmental Protection Agency, and brand-new toxicity regulations.[6]

By the 1970s and 1980s, science brought environmental crises into view. We began to see our environment through this lens, realizing that our advances were maybe not so advanced after all. Our reliance on vehicles contributed to an energy crisis.

---

5   Aldo Leopold, *A Sand County Almanac, and Sketches Here and There* (1949; repr., New York: Oxford University Press, 1989).

6   "The US Federal Government Responds," Environment and Society Portal, http://www.environmentandsociety.org/exhibitions/silent-spring/us-federal-government-responds.

Our agricultural practices spiked water pollution. Our rampant development destroyed critical habitat for species. Rather than a dualistic focus on the use of or protection of nature, science helped us to see an undeniable interconnectedness. We looked to the future and saw what kind of world would be left for our children. In this context, we began to question the direct impact that we have and the ways in which our choices affect human health and survival.

Furthermore, as technology created an increasingly globalized society, we recognized that these choices extended well beyond any one nation's borders. In a 1987 report entitled "Our Common Future," the World Commission on Environment and Development focused on the global character of our environmental issues and the need to achieve "sustainable development."[7]

Today, our understanding of conservation continues to progress, with business taking center stage. Consumers are holding companies accountable for their sustainable use of resources, and many want to be receptive to science and be good stewards of the planet. The private sector has entered the conversation in a new way, recognizing the importance of reconciling that long-held conflict between use and protection. Although government and nonprofits will continue to be an integral part of the solution, corporations now have a substantial role to play.

Sustainability initiatives provide more than a social license for businesses to operate. Growing resource scarcity and degradation has a very real impact on the private sector's profitability and survival. We have a long way to go. A 2018 report from global nonprofit Business for Social Responsibility (BSR) states

---

7   World Commission on Environment and Development, *Our Common Future* (New York: Oxford University Press, 1987).

that, "while 90 percent of CEO and C-Suite leadership has significant influence over the sustainability agenda, only 40 percent of sustainability teams were prioritizing engagement with the CEO's office."[8]

A new evolution is on the horizon, but unfortunately for today's scientists, activists, and change-makers, the more specific of those fifty-year-old predictions turned out to be spectacularly wrong—just as many of our current CEOs and leaders were stepping into the beginnings of their careers. Our understanding of how to reconcile our relationship to nature is not yet fully formed. This makes it difficult for companies to know what sustainability efforts to invest in, especially if it hinders profit. When business practices become regulated based on science that doesn't seem stable, we begin to bicker and balk about the present rather than working toward a shared future.

While it's important to conserve our natural world, deepen our scientific understanding, and grow our sustainable business practices, underlying it all is a need to establish more responsive, adaptive ways of knowing and of connecting to the world and to each other. In other words, the way we approach conservation today is not and *cannot* be the way we approached it a hundred years ago.

A 2019 United Nations (UN) report on biodiversity concluded as much—arguing that as humans accelerate the extinction of other species at an unprecedented speed, there is a need for *transformational change*. The report went on to specify, "We

8   Aron Cramer, Dunstan Allison-Hope, Alison Taylor, Beth Richmond, and Charlotte Bancilhon, "Redefining Sustainable Business: Management for a Rapidly Changing World," BSR, January 29, 2018, https://www.bsr.org/en/our-insights/report-view/redefining-sustainable-business-management-for-a-rapidly-changing-world.

mean a fundamental, system-wide reorganization across technological, economic, and social factors, including paradigms, goals, and values."[9] Transactional changes are no longer enough. We cannot only campaign on behalf of the need for beautiful parks or tug on emotions with pictures of starving polar bears. We cannot think only of one place, one species, or the responsibility of one leader, organization, or sector to create change.

What we need is transformative change. We need system-wide deconstruction and reconstruction on all levels and in all facets of our behavior and operations. As with any evolution, this new paradigm will require us to adopt new thought processes, not for a single company or a single sustainability goal but for everyone.

This begs the million-dollar question: How does an *entire system* change?

I believe our next evolution—not only for conservation but arguably extending to all facets of leadership and life—will come through a practice of leadership that is centered around relationships. Put simply, we are growing beyond extraction. Protection and profits are increasingly driven by our relationship *to* the natural world, the many and varied relationships *within* the natural world, and our relationships *to ourselves and one another*.

Our epistemology is built through conscious approaches to our interconnectedness, knowing what we don't know, and acknowledging what cannot be predicted.

9   E. S. Brondizio, J. Settele, S. Díaz, and H. T. Ngo, eds., "Global Assessment Report on Biodiversity and Ecosystem Services of the Intergovernmental Science-Policy Platform on Biodiversity and Ecosystem Services," (Bonn, Germany: IPBES secretariat, 2019).

THE PREDICTIONS ARE NOT THE MOVEMENT

There were three thematic predictions that defined the environmental movement of the midtwentieth century: overpopulation and food shortages, pollution, and climate change. The rhetoric surrounding each of these threats was dire.

There were assumptions that the global population would outpace food production within ten years. Predicted threats surrounding pollution were so damning that they led to immediate legislation in the United States, such as the Endangered Species Act, followed later by the Clean Air and Clean Water Acts. Finally, while climate change was as much at the forefront of the conversation then, as it is now, predictions at that time said that the Earth was cooling. Without swift action, we were almost certainly facing another ice age.

Here we are a full generation later, and while we haven't solved overpopulation, it clearly has not ended the world. The dreaded hole in the ozone layer has begun to heal, and we know much more about it now than we did then. And about that ice age...

On its face, the desperate predictions turned out to be completely wrong. Upon closer inspection, the lesson we can take from this is one about the complex impact of public awareness and what it looks like when up-leveled societal consciousness leads to new action. When the only thing that we can predict is the constancy of change, our responsibility lies with how we respond to it.

We don't have to look to the past *or* the future to see that our world is constantly in flux and that climate is only one facet of it. Turn on the news, look out your window, or simply exist as a person in this era, and the facts are difficult to ignore.

Today, we see natural disasters—fires, flooding, windstorms, and invasive species—with greater frequency and intensity than ever before. What's more, there are segments of the population that are completely removed from the effects of these disasters, while other segments are completely devastated by them. A greater concentration of wealth has created a disparity that incubates a desire for change and creates vastly different perceptions of the world from community to community.

Within the United States specifically, we have a measurable impact on the environment that outsizes our population. Dave Tilford of the Sierra Club said, "A child born in the United States will create thirteen times as much ecological damage over the course of his or her lifetime than a child born in Brazil."[10] Now factor in the millennial generation, which is poised to be the largest American generation since the baby boomers in spite of our dropping birth rates, and that impact grows exponentially. The impact of Generation Z is yet to be seen.

As a group, millennials are the most diverse generation in history. Individuals who identify as multiracial contribute to that diversity now more than ever. As a result, their perspectives and values will influence the future of this world. Millennials are more focused on systemic change than previous generations—73 percent of millennial consumers would be willing to spend more on a product if it came from a sustainable brand, and 81 percent expect their favorite companies to make public declarations of corporate citizenship.[11]

---

10 Roddy Scheer and Doug Moss, "Use It and Lose It: The Outsize Effect of U.S. Consumption on the Environment," *Scientific American*, September 14, 2012, https://www. scientificamerican.com/article/american-consumption-habits/.

11 "The Sustainability Imperative: New Insights on Consumer Expectations," Nielsen Company, October 12, 2015, https://www.nielsen.com/us/en/insights/report/2015/ the-sustainability-imperative-2/.

There is much more change afoot than how we are voting with our dollars too. Digital disruption is upending financial institutions, women are a growing component of a shifting political leadership climate, and political movements are beginning on social networking platforms. Add global pandemics and a worldwide movement for racial equality to the mix, and it can be said—without any sense of hyperbole—that our personal, societal, and political divisions are at an all-time high.

This is what current data and observations tell us: our world is changing in every way possible and will not respond to outmoded ways of thinking, leading, and collaboration. We are more aware, more diverse, and are struggling to communicate with each other through it all.

This is where we are. Where we go from here is up to us.

A FUTURE FILLED WITH HOPE AND INTENTION

As I was writing this book, my friend's daughter graduated from high school and declared an environmental science major in college. Each concept I present is with her generation in mind: What do we need to learn now so that, when she's my age in twenty years, she will have a solid foundation to collaborate with other leaders of her time? How do we embody a form of collaborative leadership that we know is needed so that we can teach it to her generation? What do we need to change about the world so that they have a place to go rather than a mess to undo?

This brought to mind early space exploration, when humans first left the planet. After astronaut Bill Anders snapped a photo from space—the iconic image now dubbed *Earthrise*—

he famously said, "We came all this way to explore the Moon, and the most important thing is that we discovered the Earth."[12]

There they were, executing one of the biggest missions that humanity had ever undertaken—yet as they turned around to head home, it was the Earth that stood out as the most beautiful discovery. For centuries, we have looked outside of ourselves for the solutions to our environmental challenges. We sought to protect the Earth, and we learned to use and manage its resources. We found spiritual renewal, wrote legislation, called on science, and prioritized our business actions, but we did all of those things either as individuals or alongside each other. The one quest we've yet to undertake is to turn inward and toward each other.

Our most important discovery is and always will be the mysteries of this world. And we are part of that discovery. There is a well of untapped resources that exist within and between us just waiting to be found and applied.

There are no easy or definitive answers to our questions, but this is our home. Now more than ever, we recognize that we must do something drastically different to ensure an inclusive and sustainable future. The values that we hold so dear—both human and ecological—are at risk. A new form of leadership is needed. We are invited to evolve.

There are four leadership practices at the heart of our evolution. Used consistently, these practices strengthen our collaborative efforts and empower us to take collective action. I developed

---

12   "'The First Earthrise' Apollo 8 Astronaut Bill Anders Recalls the First Mission to the Moon," Museum of Flight, December 20, 2008, https://www.museumofflight.org/ News/2267/quotthe-first-earthrisequot-apollo-8-astronaut-bill-anders-recalls-the-first.

this leadership model based on years of working in collaborative spaces, first as a conservation and international development practitioner, then later as a facilitator of transformational change. I've seen the success of this model to move our shared environmental agenda forward.

THE FOUR PRACTICES

Each practice has a central question that guides leaders toward mastery of collaborative leadership. They provide guidance at all stages of our growth and help us to remember how to navigate change.

- **Cultivate Presence:** What is the compelling reason for doing this work?
- **Create Space:** How do we create environments that foster inclusive, trusting, and engaged partnerships?
- **Leverage Diversity:** What barriers need to be broken to ensure that diverse lived experiences are the fuel that ignite lasting change?
- **Sustain Dialogue:** How do we elevate our communication with one another in a way that consistently generates novel pathways to action?

TAKING COLLECTIVE ACTION

These practices create momentum and progress toward our shared vision. Collective action is more than a strategy. It's a journey of continuous learning that leverages collaborative leadership to produce innovative results.

- **Taking Collective Action:** What is the process we must follow to make substantial gains on our most pressing issues?

There is no one way to look at these practices. I present them in a linear way—the way our brains like to follow along—but you'll also notice their cyclical, sometimes simultaneous, nature. This cyclical pattern is more reflective of the collaborative leadership experience. I offer the following image as a way to think about that pattern. Collective Action is the center that holds us together, but each leadership practice is an outgrowth that reinforces our ability to lead collaboratively.

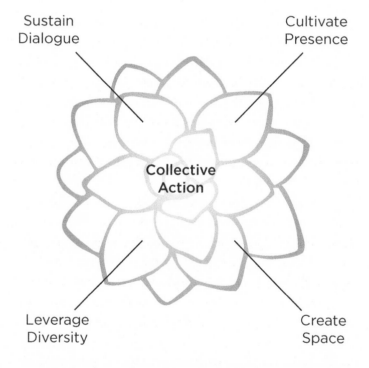

Sustain Dialogue

Cultivate Presence

Collective Action

Leverage Diversity

Create Space

In the chapters that follow, you will see that these practices begin with a personal commitment and then extend outward to how we work together within teams, organizations, partnerships, and society as a whole. They each call us toward a fundamental truth: the collective impact that our world needs can only be created through relationships—to ourselves, to each other, and to the natural world.

These are practices that I implement in my own life and embed in my work on conservation and sustainability strategies. I teach individuals, teams, and partnerships how to use them to strengthen their leadership approach and stay the course on intractable issues. They are the necessary and missing links in our ability to create a resilient, healthy, thriving planet.

Notice that I have chosen the word *practice* very intentionally.

It's easy for us to accept that things like playing the piano require skill-building over time. We don't expect a four-year-old to play Beethoven within a year of starting lessons. Yet we also recognize that in ten years, that same four-year-old may have developed an incredible mastery of the instrument, may quit altogether, or may be somewhere in between. It all depends on how much she practices.

Leadership is a practice as well. Attend all of the leadership classes and read every leadership book you want (*yes*, even this one)—and you are still only at the beginning. Excellence emerges through habit. As individuals, that means we commit to it in our daily lives and routines. In collaboration with others, that means we integrate it into our culture and processes.

Practice gives you wide permission to be imperfect. *Practice* means learning is in process and that you'll almost certainly strike a few wrong keys along the way. And *practice* is required by everyone—even if you're a master pianist or an incredibly mindful leader.

Some of the principles are going to challenge you, your organizations, and your partnerships. Each of them is grounded in ways that are practical, applicable, and directly connected to results. However, this book isn't a formula, nor does it promise immediate results.

You should also be aware that there is nothing here that you can measure definitively by numbers. You'll feel and see the difference before anything else, and in a world that's increasingly hungry for connection, that measurement should be celebrated. For those who are already saying, "That will never work for me," hang tight. I'll give you some very scientific reasons about why it will. There is a body of leadership research that shows a statistically significant tie between the leadership effectiveness gained through these practices and organizational performance.

As you join me in this effort, please trust that you are far ahead of much of the world in your readiness. Having worked with thousands of leaders, I know that people who have a love and appreciation of the natural world tend toward an intuitive understanding of how to apply what I will share with you in these pages. There is something about the time we have spent in nature, our knowledge and observation of its inner workings, the stillness it provides, the awe it inspires, and all of its wonder that has primed us for this deep, transformative leadership work.

Lastly, the full impact and intent of this book is only partially for the people who will read it. In fact, any leadership work is only partially for us. At the heart of it all, our evolution as leaders creates a world that's adaptable to the change that will inevitably happen. That resilience extends beyond our natural resources, to our ecosystems, and to society.

I posit that the necessary next steps in collaboration and our leadership evolution is not to restore ourselves to a point in time but to value the undeniable intersections we have with one another *and* our natural world in a way that completely reshapes our future.

Fifty years ago, we celebrated Earth Day for the first time. Fifty years from now, the children who are born this year will be the adults contending with the planet we leave for them. Let's rise to the occasion, like the Earth rose over the Moon that famous day in space. We can leave them with more than what we have now. It's time to embrace and challenge our differences, to learn together, to work together, to act together, and to *be* together.

This is what collaborative leadership looks like. And this is our next evolution.

Part One

THE EVOLUTION
WITHIN

Chapter One

THE CALL FOR TRANSFORMATION

There is no death, only a change of worlds.

—CHIEF SEATTLE, SUQUAMISH TRIBE

I grew up in the Sonoran Desert. I watched in wonder as beautiful monsoon storms rolled through every July and August. I saw the saguaro cactus burst into fantastic white blooms in late spring. I absorbed the rain-like smell of creosote bushes as I explored the vast desert that was my backyard. When I close my eyes, I can still bring that smell to mind today. I observed the ebb and flow of a stark landscape that was highly adapted to its environment. Put simply, I fell in love with nature. And that connection to the planet shaped my interests and concerns on a very formative level throughout my life.

When I was in elementary school, there was a category in the science fair for innovation. At the time, six-pack rings were the plastic straws of today. The media flooded the news with images of seabirds being strangled by this commonplace, single-use invention. I was worried, and I had to do something about it.

The project I chose was comically dangerous: I created a device constructed of Exacto knife blades on hinged blocks of wood, perfectly positioned so that you could slice through the six-pack rings with a single motion. The goal was to make it easy for people to cut the rings all at once rather than needing to pull out their scissors to snip them one by one. I figured that can crushers had encouraged people to recycle aluminum. Why not make a simple device for plastic rings too?

Needless to say, my block full of blades did not win.

My childhood inclinations toward environmentalism were not stayed by the loss, however. I continued to absorb messages of the eighties and nineties: "Save the rainforest," "Save the whales," "Heal the ozone." They weren't just buzzwords or campaigns to me. When I wasn't making deathtrap science experiments, I was adopting endangered species or harassing my poor mother over her aerosol hair sprays. This was serious business. I was deeply connected to the world around me, concerned about its future, and felt called from a young age to be part of the solution.

When it was time to head off to college, my university—Arizona State—was one of a handful of schools federally funded to pilot a bachelor of science in "biology and society." It was in good company among a handful of ivy leagues, including Cornell and Stanford. The program was designed for students who wanted to combine biological sciences with contemporary social, ecological, political, and ethical issues.

It was a unique way to begin my education and exposed me to leading researchers in this field whose work still impacts me today. I was mentored by an amazing group of thought leaders and scientists. They immediately took me into their research projects that focused on collaborative approaches to conservation.

Just shy of my nineteenth birthday, I found myself in Mexico City studying community-based conservation in the last *ejido*—communally owned land—within the limits of one of the largest, most rapidly developing cities in the world. For four years, I worked with the local community, Mexican university professors, domestic and international nongovernmental organizations, a global private-sector leader in the building materials industry, and city planning officials.

I played a role in building trust among the diverse perspectives at the table, helped to outline a vision for sustainable development in the community, and worked with everyone to design strategies that aligned to the vision. The result was the creation of a community-owned ecotourism venture. The benefits were plenty.

It allowed them to:

- retain their land against threats of development
- enhance their livelihoods
- conserve the habitat of an endemic and endangered species
- protect a watershed that served nearly twenty million residents of Mexico City
- provide recreational opportunities to an urban population craving renewal in nature

This project was the seed that would grow an entire career focused on collaborative environmental leadership. Through observation and experience, I began to catch glimpses of the way relationships influenced outcomes. By the time I left this project in 2002, I was inspired by the way that collaboration led to collective action.

The ultimate outcome of this work was not as I expected. An endangered rabbit found only in Mexico, the *zacatuche* or volcano rabbit, was the rallying point for this project. It was last seen in the wild in 2003. It was declared extinct in 2018.[13] Did we fail? Were we too late? Had I known how the story ended, would my inspiration have been extinguished alongside the *zacatuche*?

It wouldn't have. It would have spurred me on.

---

13 "Volcano Rabbit Declared Extinct Due to Loss of Habitat," *Mexico Daily News*, September 29, 2018, https://mexiconewsdaily.com/news/volcano-rabbit-declared-extinct-due-to-lost-habitat/.

After Mexico, I was driven to learn how others throughout the world approached collaborative conservation initiatives. With a dual major in Spanish and an emphasis in Latin American studies, I spent most of my university years abroad. I wrote grants to study community-based conservation. Ecuador, Guatemala, and Brazil became my next playgrounds. I also found myself living in Kenya midway between Amboseli and Tsavo National Parks, negotiating the complexities of community wildlife management. I sailed between villages in Thailand interfacing with communities and industry on sustainable fisheries. And long before climate change was apparent elsewhere, I was working in the Pacific on the impact of sea-level rise on small island nations.

The issues that had seemed so big to me in Arizona took a back seat to the scale of problems that plagued the places I was working. Poverty, lack of education, gender equality, child mortality, HIV/AIDS, malaria, social justice—environmental issues were tied into everything. I couldn't study conservation without appreciating the intersection of the entire system.

I witnessed firsthand the awakening that businesses were having about natural resource sustainability, access to water, soil erosion, and deforestation. I listened as communities struggled in the face of resource degradation and poverty, seeking alternatives that would create natural and economic prosperity. I was brought into the practice of solving these issues by governmental and nongovernmental organizations—the entities that most often served to convene all of these stakeholders for collaboration. My own consciousness was evolving, and my understanding of conservation was becoming more holistic.

The questions I became increasingly interested in answering

were not ones of siloed concern but whether we could find solutions at these crossroads:

- How do we work together to create positive environmental outcomes while also addressing critical social and economic issues?
- What will it require of leaders in all sectors?
- How do we get there?

These questions drew me back to the Pacific Islands, where the dynamics felt most acute to me at the time. I obtained my master's degree in the multidisciplinary area of development studies from Victoria University in New Zealand. When I finally lifted my head up after years of being abroad, I realized that these issues were growing back home. I returned to the United States, where I spent ten years of my career working with the U.S. Forest Service. A federal land management agency responsible for the nation's forests and grasslands, the Forest Service sharpened my political savvy and put me at the center of a broad array of collaborative—and sometimes not so collaborative—initiatives.

Now five years into my private consulting practice and with all of these varied experiences under my belt, I still believe these questions are worth answering—and more and more of the world agrees.

SIGNALS OF A SHIFTING SOCIETY

Thankfully, from the time of my awkward little science fair project through my college years and beyond, others were taking the changing, intersecting issues of society and the environment seriously too—people with much greater influence than I had at the time.

In 1992, representatives from all over the world gathered in Rio de Janeiro to form a multilateral treaty through the Convention on Biological Diversity. Global nongovernmental organizations like Conservation International brought science, policy, and business together under a singular umbrella. Their work paved the way for novel approaches to environmental and economic issues in an interdependent context. Scientists, nongovernmental organizations, and government officials were elevating the messages that connected human behavior to negative environmental impact—how a love for mahogany could deforest the lungs of the Earth, or how something as simple as those plastic rings or everyday hair products could endanger species or the planet itself.

In 2000, the UN brought together representatives from over one thousand organizations and more than one hundred countries to develop the Millennium Development Goals. The international community agreed to focus on poverty alleviation, environmental protection, human rights, and protection of vulnerable populations. The solutions centered around developed countries providing resources and financing for poorer countries to accomplish the agreed-upon goals.

At the time, it was a groundbreaking step for the global community to establish shared objectives. Of the eight goals developed, environmental sustainability showed up as the seventh. Fifteen years later, the UN convened to update the Millennium Development Goals and created the Sustainable Development Goals for 2015–2030. The shift in the way the goals are written demonstrates heightened understanding of the inextricable link between our environmental, social, and economic issues. Instead of the environment being a single pillar of focus, it's viewed as part of a framework of seventeen goals that cannot be separated.

The Sustainable Development Goals also emphasize shared responsibility between developed and developing countries to achieve them. It's a pivot in approach that acknowledges that everyone must participate, engage, and collaborate as we reach for success. The process for developing and adopting these goals was a collaborative effort in and of itself with stakeholders around the world determining the agenda for the next fifteen years. It took this level of participation to ensure that 191 countries would commit to address our challenges collectively.

We cannot accomplish goals as lofty as those in front of us if we move through them one by one. We cannot reduce poverty without sustainability. We cannot address complexity without connectedness.

And we cannot be satisfied with anything less than complete systemic change.

A NEW FRONTIER FOR COLLABORATION

One of the community-based conservation projects that I worked on in Brazil was the development of a supply chain for açaí fruit from the rural communities of the Amazon Basin to the burgeoning urban areas of Manaus and Belém. Although you can now have your own bowl of açaí in almost any major metropolitan area in the United States, at the time of this project in 2000, you would have been hard-pressed to find it anywhere except in the Amazonian communities where it had been a dietary staple for generations. An economic opportunity was born—not out of an American superfood craze but as a result of the *ribeirinho*, or "river people," migrating to the city in search of jobs. They had left their homes but not their cultural or gastronomic disposition for the fruit.

There was an environmental impetus for this project as well. Açaí grows on palm trees. These are the same palms that are widely used for palm oil and harvesting hearts of palm. At the time, both of these uses were more profitable and less sustainable than açaí production. Since açaí is a tree fruit, its harvest doesn't require the complete felling of the tree. Rather, the *ribeirinhos* pluck the berries that grow naturally throughout the forest. Their cultivation methods also include agroforestry practices reliant on intact rainforest ecosystems to protect against soil erosion. Producing palm oil or hearts of palm, on the other hand, often requires that the trees become traditional crops, which results in deforestation to make way for intensive planting.

All things considered, the tactical formula for this project was overwhelmingly straightforward. A new market for açaí already existed among the growing population in nearby urban areas. There were specific communities where the fruit grew in sustainable quantities and mostly wild conditions. Our work was to connect all the points along the supply chain. Points, I might add, that were already established to sell palm oil and hearts of palm. The approach to this socioeconomic conservation challenge was not uncommon for its era. Although we were addressing the larger systemic issue of deforestation in the Amazon, we were doing it in a hyperlocalized way focused on a narrow slice of the system.

One by one, I worked with communities and a Brazilian university to flesh out the opportunity. First and foremost, I led each community through a participatory mapping process that allowed them to represent visually what was most important to them within the community. They drew a map of their land, indicating the areas and landmarks that were of meaning to them: the forest, the soccer field, the schools, the river, and more.

As we explored the map together, their community values rose to the surface. This happened well before we developed any plan or strategy. Through the process of mapping and dialogue, they were able to express the vision that they had for their community and the purpose behind engaging in the açaí cultivation project.

Although the economic incentives were important, there was more at stake. Stable sources of income from sustainable practices on their land allowed them to preserve that which was most important to them. Participating in this project meant they could remain in their communities rather than leave for the city, have additional resources to educate their children, and maintain the values that were integral to their quality of life. Among those values was a connection with a healthy, thriving forest.

We worked backward from the point of distribution to the community to ensure fair wages: from the plant that processed the fruit, to the local entrepreneur who sold it to the plant, to the boat captain that carried the fruit up the river, to the *ribei-rinho* who harvested it. Sustainability was key to this effort, not because I was driving my own conservation agenda but because the community had theirs. They understood the long-term economic and ecological benefits to their approach.

Since that time, market demand for açaí has grown globally. By a stroke of luck, the American founders of Sambazon—the largest international producer and distributor of açaí—built their company on solid ethics. They are committed to maintaining the integrity of the forest and the communities that depend on it. They are certified fair trade, work with nongovernmental partners like the World Wildlife Fund (WWF) to ensure açaí is harvested sustainably, and have maintained the community-based character of production by supporting independent local growers.[14]

While the açaí project was successful in its own right, it was not sufficient. The threat and impacts of deforestation in the Amazon continue. The fires that raged through the region in 2019, the worst on record, are evidence of that. The Amazon rainforest extends across nine countries with different cultures, laws, and regulations. Logging and cattle production are still more economically viable options, including in areas where açaí is not native. Agriculture remains Brazil's strongest performing sector of the economy. Political divisiveness flares egos and starts trade wars. Both impact the types of industries that prevail.

As Brazil wrestled with how it would respond to the fires, the

---

14 Gina-Marie Cheeseman, "How Sustainability Is Embedded in Sambazon," *The Guardian*, December 1, 2010, https://www.theguardian.com/sustainable-business/sustainability-sambazon-embedded-certification-acai.

rest of the world chimed in with its opinions and asked the question, "Who owns the Amazon?"[15] Is it the landowner, the government, a collection of nations, or all of us? No matter what the answer, the potential implications are daunting.

Resolving the complexity of this issue and others like it's a massive undertaking. It involves social, political, and economic factors on top of the obvious environmental ones. The days of focusing on *one* product or *one* issue within *one* community that meet *one* need are long gone. Small-scale collaborations like those fostered by the açaí project can only be part of the answer in a much larger, more integrated web. We don't have the time or financial resources to invest in anything other than new forms of collaboration at an unprecedented scale.

TRANSACTIONAL AND RELATIONAL COLLABORATION

We have understood collaboration in different ways over time. It has always been present in our response to environmental challenges, but how we have engaged with it has evolved much in line with our consciousness. I began this book with the story of John Muir and Teddy Roosevelt. One might view their camping trip, in some fashion, as a form of collaboration. But in Roosevelt's position of presidential leadership, his decisions were unilateral even though there was arguably public support for the outcomes they yielded.

We are entering a new frontier of collaboration. Transactional collaboration, where a single bill could sign a national park into existence, is giving way to relational collaboration, where

---

15   Meg Kelly and Sarah Cahlan, "The Brazilian Amazon Is Still Burning. Who Is Responsible," *Washington Post*, October 7, 2019, https://www.washingtonpost.com/politics/2019/10/07/brazilian-amazon-is-still-burning-who-is-responsible/.

everyone feels they have some ownership of entire ecosystems thousands of miles away. We are also shifting away from outcomes that are narrow to ones that are systemic. What was once a cry to "Save the rainforest!" is now a much more complex, less geographically identifiable need to address carbon emissions and sequestration. The role that forests play is just one part of the equation. And carbon? It's a villain we can't even see.

That isn't to say that transactional or narrow solutions don't provide some benefit. But we recognize the potential for more, and we are on the cusp of understanding the leadership it will take to get there. On the cusp but not yet arrived.

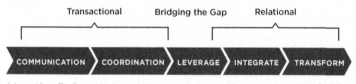

Adapted from *The Partnership Institute's Maximizing the Impact of Partnerships for the SDGs* (2018)

There isn't a universally agreed upon definition of collaboration within this new paradigm. But there tend to be similar stages of growth. At one end of the spectrum lies *communication* and *coordination.* These are the transactional types of collaboration focused on narrow issues. They tend to be characterized by one-way and opportunistic interactions with limited alignment among partners.

The bridge to relational collaboration comes in the form of *leveraging* resources to accomplish a shared goal. Partners acknowledge the interdependence of their work and actively work together. They openly exchange knowledge, skills, technology, and funding that helps achieve the desired outcome. Through this process, relationships begin to strengthen."

At the far end of the spectrum lie *integration* and *transformation*. These are fully relational forms of collaboration and have the potential to deliver the systemic impact that we so desperately need. They share an essential key characteristic: dialogue. Dialogue also happens to be one of the leadership practices we will explore later on in the book. Stay tuned.

RELATIONAL FORMS OF COLLABORATION

In my work, I guide clients through the stages of *leveraging, integrating*, and *transforming*. The following table exemplifies how value is created through these three forms of collaborative partnership development:

LEVERAGE/EXCHANGE	INTEGRATE/COMBINE	TRANSFORM
One partner contributes to the work of another, or partners exchange resources, to allow one or both partners to deliver more.	Two or more partners combine their resources together to deliver more than each could deliver alone.	Multiple actors work together through collective action to tackle complex challenges, usually through system transformation.
Often transactional, one-way transfer or reciprocal exchange of skills, knowledge, funding, etc. Involves negotiation to maximize the gains on both sides.	Characterized by cogeneration, mutual accountability, and innovative approaches. Involves brainstorming and creative dialogue to together develop new approaches that create value.	Involves multiple actors bringing together unique and complementary resources, all essential pieces of a jigsaw puzzle. Requires multistakeholder dialogue to understand the system and engage the players required to make interventions
VALUE CREATED:	**VALUE CREATED:**	**VALUE CREATED:**
ORGANIZATIONAL VALUE	**ORGANIZATIONAL VALUE**	**ORGANIZATIONAL VALUE**
	MISSION VALUE	**MISSION VALUE**

LEVERAGE/EXCHANGE	INTEGRATE/COMBINE	TRANSFORM
Applicable when:	**Applicable when:**	**Applicable when:**
Each partner has something that is more valuable to the other than to themselves, resulting in net gain on exchange.	Bringing together complementary resources results in new approaches that deliver value to all.	An issue is sufficiently complex that a systems approach is required to tackle it.
Example:	**Example:**	**Example:**
Coca-Cola and the Global Fund's Project Last Mile leverages Coca-Cola's logistic, supply chain, distribution, and marketing expertise to build African governments' capabilities to ensure communities have better access to life-sustaining and life-enhancing medicines. Coca-Cola gains by demonstrating its commitment to a better planet, as well as providing employee engagement opportunities.	SOLShare/Grameen Shakti's Smart Peer-to-Peer Solar Grids for Rural Electrification & Empowerment is a Bangladesh-based partnership between a social enterprise, SOLShare, and a major supplier of renewable energy, Grameen Shakti, which is being supported and enabled by UN DESA. Grameen Shakti brings access to its massive existing customer base and network of solar homes, as well as its knowledge of the communities. SOLShare brings cutting-edge, innovative technology with the potential to transform the supply of affordable energy to low-income households in Bangladesh.	Scaling Up Nutrition (SUN) is a global, country-led, and multisectoral movement to combat undernutrition and catalyze support for countries to "scale up nutrition," with a focus on a set of evidence-based direct nutrition interventions. At country level, multisector (e.g., ministries of education, health, and agriculture) as well as multistakeholder collaborative action (including business, civil society, and the UN) are facilitated to deliver system change.

Source: Darian Stibbe, Stuart Reid, and Julia Gilbert, "Maximising the Impact of Partnerships for the SDGs: A Practical Guide to Partnership Value Creation," United Nations Department of Economic and Social Affairs (UNDESA), 2019, https://sustainabledevelopment.un.org/index.php?page=view&type=400&nr=2564&menu=35.

As you move progressively from *communication* toward *transformation*, there is an increasing amount of trust and relationship required between partners. Partners must invest more time and resources to achieve their shared goals. With more investments comes an increased risk of failure. But the reward that success brings is a multifold increase in impact.

While the idea of collaboration is not a hard sell, putting it into practice is. The bigger the change, the more difficult it is to work together to accomplish it. It's hard to protect individual goals in the process. To get to transformational collaboration, all parties must adopt a mindset of creating value together that ultimately impacts systemic change. In some instances, that may mean letting go of short-term gains to ensure long-term impact. Learning how to do this requires a different set of leadership skills like the ones presented in later chapters.

Transformational collaboration allows us to grow our impact by rethinking how we create value. As our relationships and trust strengthen, so does our ability to deconstruct the systems that stand in our way of social and environmental sustainability.

"RETHINKING THE TRIPLE BOTTOM LINE THROUGH A SYSTEMS LENS"

(Future-Fit Foundation, 2017)

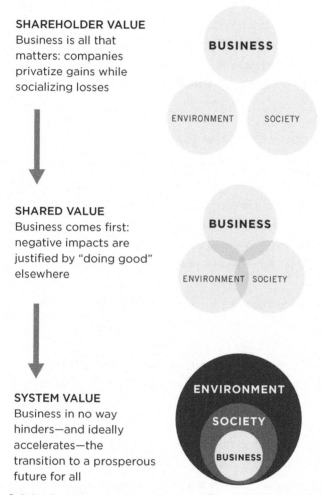

SHAREHOLDER VALUE
Business is all that matters: companies privatize gains while socializing losses

SHARED VALUE
Business comes first: negative impacts are justified by "doing good" elsewhere

SYSTEM VALUE
Business in no way hinders—and ideally accelerates—the transition to a prosperous future for all

Rethinking the triple bottom line through a systems lens (Future-Fit Foundation, 2017)

If we are deliberate and intentional, every effort we make is progress toward a better future. Maybe my project in the Amazon served as a proof of concept of what's possible. Or maybe it was a foreshadowing of the increasing intricacies we will have to untangle. Either way, today's challenges are best addressed as experiments—acknowledging that we do not know what we don't know and that we must take imperfect and collective action. We can fully expect changes, refinement, and even failure. And we can develop collaborative approaches that allow for adaptation. This is the way to propel ourselves down the path to a more resilient future.

FACING COMPLEXITY AND SCALE

One of my current clients has set an audacious goal:

> By 2060 we will have created the enabling conditions needed to conserve 245 million acres of remaining southern forests and their inherent social, economic, and ecological values for the benefit of current and future generations.

It's a mouthful, no? Let me break it down.

This "client" is actually a coalition of forty leaders from all three sectors: business, government, and nongovernmental organizations. In 2016, they came together concerned about the current and projected loss of forests in the southeastern United States. Each one of them has a vested stake in a healthy, connected network of forests in the region. From Georgia Pacific to The Nature Conservancy to the U.S. Forest Service and more, their missions are inextricably tied to forests and the values they provide.

The year 2060 might seem far away. Many of the people currently engaged in this effort will be long past retirement by the time that date rolls around. They are working toward a goal they may never see achieved. With the scope of influence represented by the partners in this project, individual organizations could easily have created a smaller goal that could be achieved on a shorter time frame. So, what is the impetus for such boldness?

Let's put the goal in perspective.

Two hundred forty-five million acres is roughly the same land base as one-tenth of the United States. Considering that more than 80 percent of southern forests are in the hands of private landowners,[16] there is a population of diverse stakeholders who will have a significant say in what happens to that land. Not dissimilar from the challenges I addressed in the Amazon, the fate of the resource rests in the hands of people who need economic incentives to keep their forests as forests.

Urban areas in the region are predicted to double by 2060,[17] which could easily motivate forest landowners to sell to developers for the right price. Conversion of forest to other land use will have implications for air quality, water quality, and carbon sequestration for nearly 220 million future southeastern residents. And there's economic impact too. Southern forest products contribute $260 billion to the global economy.[18]

16   Brett J. Butler and David N. Wear, "Forest Ownership Dynamics of Southern Forests," in *The Southern Forest Futures Project: Technical Report* (Asheville, NC: Southern Research Station, 2013), 103–121, https://www.fs.usda.gov/treesearch/pubs/44199.

17   Adam Terando and Vic Hines, "Scientists Predict Massive Urban Growth, Creation of 'Megalopolis' in Southeast in Next 45 Years," Department of the Interior, US Geological Survey, July 28, 2014, https://www.usgs.gov/news/scientists-predict-massive-urban-growth-creation-megalopolis-southeast-next-45-years.

18   Craig Hanson, Logan Yonavjak, Caitlin Clarke, Susan Minnemeyer, Lauriane Boisrobert, Andrew Leach, and Karen Schleeweis, "Southern Forests for the Future," World Resources Institute, March 2010, https://www.wri.org/publication/southern-forests-future#:~:text=Southern%20Forests%20for%20the%20Future%20is%20designed%20to%20serve%20as,others%20involved%20with%20forest%20stewardship..

Additionally, this area hosts a global biodiversity hotspot.[19] The North American Coastal Plain is one of only thirty-six hotspots in the world, identified as the Earth's most biologically diverse yet threatened terrestrial areas. Habitat loss is advancing rapidly. Species are at risk that exist nowhere else in the world.

The point is clear: the only way to create impact is to examine the issue holistically, systemically, and with the acceptance that the lasting solutions are multidimensional. Forty years isn't a lot of time to turn the tide on something this rapidly changing.

My client has already taken a radically different path to gain the commitment of a multisector alliance. When I was brought into this project, the initial champions of the effort imagined that the collaboration might look more like *leveraging* the resources of the group. By the end of our first several meetings, they were rallying around a vision that was in the spirit of *transforming*. The journey from 2016 until now has sometimes been bumpy and stalled out. Other times, it has been smooth and accelerated. On my part, all of it has been expected. My twenty years of experience guiding efforts like these have taught me that this is what it looks like when a group digs in to do *real* collaborative work.

When they signed on to work with one another, I don't think they knew they were signing on to learn a new form of leadership. I don't think they expected to be stretched to redefine collaboration in the way that they have. Quite honestly, I sometimes wonder if they can see how their leadership has evolved

---

19 As defined by the Critical Ecosystem Partnership Fund, a biodiversity hotspot must meet two strict criteria: it must have at least 1,500 vascular plants as endemics—which is to say, it must have a high percentage of plant life found nowhere else on the planet; it must have 30 percent or less of its original natural vegetation. In other words, hotspots are irreplaceable and threatened.

to the point where it's their relationship to one another that is the "solution" that they've been seeking all along. The quality of that relationship is what will position them for success. Now at the point of implementing strategies, some of the gnashing of teeth and frustration that surrounded the start of the project has abated. At the start of the project, many wondered aloud, "When are we going to do something?" They could hear the clock ticking ever closer to 2060.

However, it was the time they took to practice collaborative leadership that led them to more solid ground. I've played a role in getting them to this point, but they are the ones who stayed committed to learning a new way of leading. This will serve them well as they enter the next phase of the project. They will undoubtedly face trials along their road, but no matter what comes, they have built the foundation for relational collaboration.

There are very few of my clients—and very few collaborative initiatives—that begin their partnership by talking about what it means to lead collaboratively. Their challenges are pressing, their desire to make an immediate difference is high, and they all have priorities competing for their attention. In the end though, the difference between success and failure is whether collaborations take the time to learn to lead together.

Recognizing that collaborative leadership isn't yet part of our vernacular or common skillsets, I embed the four leadership practices within my engagements. The practices that I present in this book are integral to the work that we do, though my mission is to make it a more explicit and visible part of collaboration.

What results from these practices is that my clients begin

to work with one another mindfully and intentionally. They become willing to see different perspectives or challenge one another healthily. They intuitively began to use dialogue skills as a pathway to co-create new possibilities. They take collective action that yields lasting results because, through the process of collaboration, they have learned how to align and adapt under constantly changing circumstances.

To keep up with the complexity and pace of our world, we must grow as leaders. We are leaning on old models of leadership that focus on individual and hierarchical structures. In the framework of collaborative leadership, it's personal growth that serves collective growth. It's collective growth that enables us to create high-performance collaboration. And it's high-performance collaboration that allows us to be flexible and creative when confronted by unforeseen variables and challenges. In essence, collaborative leadership creates a multiplier effect.

What would be different if the next time you walked into a room, everyone was operating at their highest potential as a leader? What if that potential was amplified by the support of other leaders? How might that accelerate our ability to create transformative change?

The answers to these questions will only come once we commit to our development as collaborative leaders.

ILLUMINATING THE PATH FORWARD

I am struck by this seemingly obvious truth: any issue that we face could be solved if we focused our collective efforts toward it.

We have more than enough financial, technological, and innovative capabilities. I truly believe that. What we lack is an equally sophisticated understanding of how to be in relationship to one another so that we *can* and are *willing to* solve any problem. We know that we need to collaborate in order to achieve solutions at scale. What we don't always know is how to use the power of relationship to make that happen.

Therein lies the paradox we must resolve and the final aspect of the call for transformation. Elon Musk might agree.

In 2014, Musk released the patents on Tesla Motor's technology for electric vehicles. He wrote a blog post titled "All Our Patents Belong to You" to his competitors and would-be competitors.

Here is the compelling statement he made:

> At Tesla, however, we felt compelled to create patents out of concern that the big car companies would copy our technology and then use their massive manufacturing, sales, and marketing power to overwhelm Tesla. We couldn't have been more wrong. The unfortunate reality is the opposite: electric car programs (or programs for any vehicle that doesn't burn hydrocarbons) at the major manufacturers are small to non-existent, constituting an average of far less than one percent of their total vehicle sales.

> At best, the large automakers are producing electric cars with limited range in limited volume. Some produce no zero emission cars at all.

> Given that annual new vehicle production is approaching 100 million per year and the global fleet is approximately 2 billion cars, it's impossible for Tesla to build electric cars fast enough to address the carbon crisis. By the same token, it means the market

is enormous. Our true competition is not the small trickle of non-Tesla electric cars being produced, but rather the enormous flood of gasoline cars pouring out of the world's factories every day.

We believe that Tesla, other companies making electric cars, and the world would all benefit from a common, rapidly evolving technology platform.[20]

With these words, he gave his blessing to use Tesla's patents. Anyone who wanted them could have them. It's almost a dare: *Go ahead. Make it better. Make the world better for it. Let's do it together.*

Later in 2014, the People's Climate Movement took to the streets of New York City for their first march to demand bold action on climate change. A key component of their agenda was to engage broader demographics in the movement. Their motto became, "To change everything, we need everyone." In 2015, when the Sustainable Development Goals were adopted, collaboration was frequently identified as a catalyst for change.

These are signs of the times: we need all of us, all in. Even the people we don't agree with. Even the people we don't like.

It's a lofty ambition, as is the vision for a sustainable future. Many questions remain unanswered: How do we do work together effectively? How do we scale in a way that meets the complexity and pace of change? Who do we partner with and how? Which solutions do we go forward with, and what do we do when they don't work? How do we align everyone's values around shared solutions?

---

20 Elon Musk, "All Our Patent Are Belong to You," Tesla, June 12, 2014, https://www.tesla.com/blog/all-our-patent-are-belong-you.

As you develop mastery of the leadership practices in this book, the answers will reveal themselves. You will intuitively know how to approach even your most daunting situations. You'll be able to engage more productively with your team, organization, and a range of partners. You'll know how to execute on your vision with greater precision. You'll be more at ease with change, take more risks, and be willing to fail in the process. It's undeniable that these practices will impact your everyday life too. My hope is that your days will be filled with much more creativity and less reactivity.

This isn't a shortcut. There are none. We must do the work to become more conscious leaders, especially in service of collaboration. Collaborative leadership is conscious leadership. We are being called to a deeper understanding of ourselves and one another. It's in those depths that we will discover the power of our capacity to create change—*real* change.

With every step forward, we illuminate the path to our shared future.

Chapter Two

LINKING CONSCIOUSNESS AND COLLABORATIVE LEADERSHIP

No problem can be solved from the same level of consciousness that created it.

—ALBERT EINSTEIN, NOBEL PRIZE LAUREATE
AND SCIENCE PHILOSOPHER

One cannot live the afternoon of life according to the program of life's morning; for what was great in the morning will be of little importance in the evening, and what in the morning was true will at evening become a lie.

—CARL JUNG, FOUNDER OF ANALYTIC PSYCHOLOGY
AND THEORIES OF THE COLLECTIVE UNCONSCIOUS

Our ability to create change depends on our conscious interpretation of the world. Whether the change we seek is personal (like a desire to be healthier) or societal (like a desire for the sustainability of our planet's resources), our minds are the most powerful tool we have. The more complex the problem, the more complex our minds need to be to solve it. Desire, motivation, and discipline are not enough. To deliver lasting results on our most wicked challenges requires us to change our minds—literally.

We're just arriving at a point in our culture where the idea of "consciousness" isn't solely the domain of spiritual gurus. It can't come soon enough. There are no easy answers left. We've picked all the low-hanging fruit. Now we're left staring up from the base of the tree thinking, "How the hell am I going to get up there?" We can't see the shape, color, or size of the fruit. We don't know if there are even any to pick. And there is no ladder high enough—yet—to climb it. We not only have to develop new ways to solve problems, but we also have to develop definitions for them. Progress, let alone success, requires a new level of mental sophistication.

If this sounds daunting, consider that you've been at the base of this tree before. Over the course of your life, you have faced any number of challenges that, at the time, seemed unpredictable and uncertain. To solve the problem in front of you required that you tap into the wealth of potential that every mind possesses. Every time you did so successfully, you heightened your consciousness.

Let me explain.

Consciousness develops over time—we can see this by watching children grow. From the time that an infant comes into the world, we celebrate their growth milestones.

From birth to age two, we see them understand their surroundings through their senses. They learn to differentiate mom from dad by sight, touch, smell, and sound. They know that smashed peas taste bad and sweet blueberries taste good. They begin to crawl and walk, driven to learn movement so that they can navigate their world and their desires. And they learn that when you hide their favorite toy behind your back, it still exists.

We marvel as young children activate their imagination, when they believe in Santa Claus and play make-believe. No place is too boring to come to life as a distant kingdom. There is an open sense of possibility that motivates their exploration. Even when we're long past that sense of wonder ourselves, we protect it for them. We play their games and foster their beliefs as long as that magic exists. That's important too. It helps them to learn to think abstractly, to hold multiple ideas in their minds at once, and to use language to construct story.

As they continue to grow, logic and reason kick in. They pick up books on dinosaurs and can distinguish them from unicorns. They understand concepts in a more concrete way and become fascinated with how things work. Reality becomes something they can see and touch. Their curiosity is directed toward facts and formulas. They develop friendships and learn to differentiate themselves from their family members and peers. They understand reciprocity—that there are certain ways of behaving that hurt other people and certain rules of behavior that make friendships work.

Into teenage years, advanced ways of thinking, questioning, and hypothesizing come into play. They learn which rules to keep and which to break. They test their predictions (however poor) of the outcomes of their decisions. They question authority as they begin to stake out their own identity and code of ethics. If you're the parent of a teenager, take heart: this is all essential on the path toward more highly developed consciousness. These experiments will lead them to be original thinkers. Eventually they will move away from purely self-serving decision-making to apply their thoughts more globally.

All of these stages of cognitive development are essential. They build upon one another. While each stage of development is progressively higher in functionality, you never lose the lessons of the past. For example, even *you* can still play in an imaginary world—whether it's one a child invites you into or one you dream up on your own. You can plan the concrete steps to make dinner or plot out a road trip for your next vacation. And you engage in complex reasoning when you think about how much to invest in your 401(k) every year in order to enjoy retirement.

These are the well-recognized phases of advanced mental complexity and growing consciousness. They are easy to spot because we have firsthand experience of them in our early life and examples all around us in our children. And, as described here, they are largely tied to the physical development that progresses with chronological age.

So, what happens after our brains and bodies stop growing? Is that the end of the road for higher-ordered thinking? Do we still have the ability to create new pathways and make different decisions when confronted with ever-more-difficult situations? Or are we doomed to stay fixed in the capabilities of our midtwenties, forever adding new knowledge, data, technology, and experiences but never being able to use them to their full capacity?

We are not doomed.

Neuroscience helps us make visible the once-elusive thing we call consciousness. Research shows that we can continue our growth, branching out into bigger, deeper concepts as we move through our lives. Studies into brain plasticity demonstrate that we can shift our mindset and behaviors. We can change what we believe, how we think, the habitual ways those beliefs and thoughts influence our actions, and—in turn—become capable of interacting with the world in different, impactful ways.

This is not given to us as easily in adulthood as in childhood. Although science is still untangling the stages of adult development, we know more now than ever before. We are also living in a time that demands that more of us commit to our personal and collective growth. Upgrading our internal operating system or our consciousness is the first step to transforming collaborative leadership.

A creative genius lives in all of us. We have to work individually and together to unleash it.

CONSCIOUS MINDSETS FOR COLLABORATIVE SOLUTIONS

I began studying leadership and, more specifically, the theories behind what motivates behavioral change about ten years into my career. Throughout all of my work facilitating collaborative conservation initiatives, I noticed that there were technical solutions (e.g., creating a supply chain for açaí in the Amazon Basin) and adaptive solutions (e.g., finding an economic incentive in balance with the social and cultural values of the community).

I had worked internationally and domestically on a range of issues from endangered species to deforestation to climate change and beyond. Together with the people I served, we developed solutions that also addressed social needs in cross-cultural settings. There was one thing that stood out in each of my projects: the adaptive solutions were the grease for success.

It was about this time during my own consciousness evolution that I attended a conference hosted by the University of Michigan's Center for Positive Organizations. I was particularly fascinated by a presenter who articulated what I intuitively sensed: the point at which consciousness shifts is when something becomes so painful that it no longer can be ignored or when something becomes so purposeful that the pursuit of it is prioritized above all else. He didn't exactly use those words though. I believe he described that pain point as a "tragic loss" and the point of purpose as a "spiritual awakening."

Well, great.

Was he saying the best way to help my clients create profound change was to incite tragedy or activate divine intervention? Or was there another way to induce new mindsets and behaviors within leaders? Certainly, there had to be a structure that allowed people to evaluate what's lying beneath the surface of their resistance to change and gradually respond with new choices. I zeroed in what he was saying and reinterpreted it: the leverage points for change are the difference between technical and adaptive challenges.

Let's step back into some definitions before we go any further. Understanding the differences between technical and adaptive challenges is key. The differences emphasize the mindsets required of twenty-first century collaborative leaders.

A *technical challenge* is one where the problem is identifiable and routine. It can be resolved easily because there is existing knowledge and expertise to address it. Relationships and roles are clearly defined. The drive is to restore order as quickly as possible. And the "right people" are happily engaged in making that happen.

An *adaptive challenge* is one where the problem is ill-defined and nonroutine. It requires innovation, learning, and new thinking. The people engaged must grow their capabilities to find solutions. Competing perspectives bring into question their deeply held beliefs and values. Intensity creates new relationship dynamics, often difficult. And ingrained patterns that may have brought success in the past are difficult to break. As you might imagine, this is countered by resistance.

A simplistic example of the difference between these two challenges is someone with high blood pressure. It could be seen as either a technical or adaptive challenge. If viewed as technical, the solution would be for the person to take blood pressure medicine and call it a day. If viewed as adaptive, the solution would require that same person to commit to a lifestyle of healthy eating and exercise. Both solutions get at the problem. Both solutions may even be necessary. But one creates enduring, impactful, and systemic change.

If that's the case, why do we gravitate toward viewing the challenges before us as technical? More often than not, we come at problems looking for the quick-fix solution. Ronald Heifetz, a foremost authority on leadership who codeveloped the adaptive leadership framework, makes it clear:

> Holding on to past assumptions, blaming authority, scapegoating, externalizing the enemy, denying the problem, jumping to conclusions, or finding a distracting issue may restore stability and feel less stressful than facing and taking responsibility for a complex challenge. These patterns of response to disequilibrium are called work avoidance mechanisms and are similar to defensive routines that operate in individuals, small groups and organizations.[21]

Avoidance is easier than work. Sticking with what we know is easier than changing our mind. "Staticity" is simpler than plasticity. Unconsciousness trumps consciousness. That is, until purpose overshadows pain. When we connect to our deepest purpose, the blinders come off. The beauty of this shift in our perspective can be summed up in a quote by Anaïs Nin: "And the day came when the risk to remain tight in a bud was more painful than the risk it took to blossom."

EXAMINING COLLABORATION THROUGH THE LENS OF TECHNICAL AND ADAPTIVE CHALLENGES

The following table takes the levels of collaboration presented in chapter 1 a step further. It defines leveraging, integrating, and transforming in terms of technical and adaptive challenges. The associated solutions are also noted.

---

21 Ronald A. Heifetz, *Leadership Without Easy Answers* (Cambridge, MA: Belknap Press of Harvard University Press, 1994).

LEVEL OF COLLABORATION	COLLABORATIVE APPROACH	TECHNICAL OR ADAPTIVE CHALLENGE	SOLUTION
Leverage/Exchange: One partner contributes to the work of another, or partners exchange resources to allow one or both partners to deliver more.	Often transactional, one-way transfer, or reciprocal exchange of skills, knowledge, funding, etc. Involves negotiation to maximize the gains on both sides.	**Technical:** Problem is clear.	Solution requires expert authority of preexisting knowledge.
Integrate/Combine: Two or more partners combine their resources together to deliver more than each could deliver alone.	Characterized by cogeneration, mutual accountability, and innovative approaches. Involves brainstorming and creative dialogue to together develop new approaches that create value.	**Technical & Adaptive:** Problem is clear or easily defined.	Solution requires expert authority and stakeholders to cogenerate new knowledge.
Transform: Multiple actors work together through collective action to tackle complex challenges usually through system transformation.	Involves multiple actors bringing together unique and complementary resources, all essential pieces of a jigsaw puzzle. Requires multistakeholder dialogue to understand the system and engage the players required to make interventions.	**Adaptive:** Problem requires learning and definition.	Solution requires diverse stakeholder groups to cogenerate new knowledge.

Source: Darian Stibbe, Stuart Reid, and Julia Gilbert, "Maximising the Impact of Partnerships for the SDGs: A Practical Guide to Partnership Value Creation," United Nations Department of Economic and Social Affairs (UNDESA), 2019, https://sustainabledevelopment.un.org/index. php?page=view&type=400&nr=2564&menu=35.

REWIRING OUR CONSCIOUSNESS

I found myself in a room of wildland firefighters teaching a leadership course on risk management. For them, their work is a matter of life and death. Several fatalities sparked a national response to explore different avenues of leadership training. The course wasn't meant to replace their technical learning but to give them access to new thinking and responses in the face of risk. We were coming to the close of our time together, time during which we had explored adaptive leadership and cultivating growth mindsets.

Given that their work requires decisions be made in the literal heat of the moment, they were clear that for adaptive leadership to be meaningful, they would have to practice it and see its value in their work and life. Yes, the pain and tragic loss of the fatalities had spurred the rollout of this training. But the intent of the training was to help them to identify and dislodge the limiting beliefs that were impacting critical decision-making on fires.

There is a common phrase within the community that reflects one of their core values. They say, "Everyone comes home every day." When this value is challenged by the death of one of their colleagues, it rocks and reverberates their foundation. It demonstrates that everyone does not come home every day. There are many technical solutions that are necessary in wildland firefighting. These include tighter protocols, advanced technology to model fire behavior, and safer equipment. These technical solutions heighten their sense of security until the next fatality upends it.

I took my own risk and put it out there, "What if it's not true that everyone comes home every day? What if that thought is getting in your way of making better decisions? What would necessarily have to shift in your thinking to accept that possibility? What doors might that new thinking open for you in how you stay in relationship to one another in the most intense situations you face? How you communicate? And even how you use the technical tools available to you to make better decisions?"

Talk about rocking their foundation.

My experience of them is that they are professionals of the highest caliber. Purpose already drives them. The thing that unconsciously pulls them away from that purpose is the fear of loss. They avoid the very real possibility of death. It's tricky. Many in the community would disagree with my assessment. But on that day in that room, I cracked the door open on a new level of consciousness, and just enough air got in.

I didn't have the answers to my questions. One of them did. Here's what he said:

> I drive home every night along the same route. I leave work at the same time. I know the patterns of traffic. I can get there without thinking. I *do* get there without thinking. Now, I know that something unexpected could happen. But I don't really want to think about what it would be like for my wife or my girls if something did. I guess I don't really accept that the unexpected will happen.

> I thought about this last night as I drove home. I was aware of where I was and what was happening around me. I even put the windows down so that I could hear the wind. I pictured my family in my mind. My wife said she noticed something different about me when I got home. My girls laughed more than usual at dinner.

> I don't know if that's what you mean by consciousness, how it impacts us, or how that translates to what we do on a fire. But I think you're on to something that we haven't yet realized.

Bingo.

His comment sparked authentic dialogue. I'm not saying that we changed their culture. They didn't walk out of the room with a new belief system in place. But they did challenge themselves to think differently, aware of their blind spots. They were a lot more vulnerable and honest about their personal and collective fears. They could see clearly that there was risk in holding tight to what they had always thought and done. It was the beginning of a journey to explore mindsets that would serve their ultimate purpose, which was (and is) to protect human life and natural resources.

Your challenges—and what's at risk—are likely not imminent death. But the story is illustrative. One slight change of one person's mind can have a cascading effect. It's about more than a "feel good" session. Dan Siegal, a clinical professor of psychiatry at the University of California, Los Angeles, states that insights like those that the firefighters gained that day have "the power to shape our brain's firing patterns, as well as to shape the architecture of the brain itself."[22]

When we begin to examine our habitual patterns of thought, we can see how often we respond to life on an unconscious level. In most circumstances, the neural pathways that elicit these responses are there to make our lives more efficient. But when new challenges present themselves, those old pathways get in the way of accessing new solutions. We have to interrupt neurological patterns that have likely been there for years. It's possible, but it takes time to see those patterns and practice new responses. We have to rewire the connections in our brains. As that rewire

22 Daniel J. Siegel, *Mindsight: The New Science of Personal Transformation* (New York: Bantam Books, 2010).

takes hold, we gain access to more advanced ways of defining our challenges and more complex thinking and problem-solving.

This rewiring of consciousness is hard enough to do as an individual. It becomes more difficult when whole groups of people are asked to do it together. There is, however, a level of accountability that doing this work in collaboration can provide. We can use one another to gain perspective that might otherwise be impossible to see on our own. Collaboration offers us the opportunity to learn how to think together at higher, more creative levels so that we can discover adaptive solutions. We change our mind's architecture to see the dynamics at play with greater clarity.

To be sure, the growth of our individual and collective consciousness is a lifelong pursuit. We are all in different stages and will progress at different speeds. There will be some who cannot begin the journey, and there will be some that plateau. It takes significant dedication for this work to be a cornerstone of our lives. Many don't buy into the importance of it. If you *are* bought in, it's important to be aware of this and to meet people where they are.

You may find yourself in an environment where it's difficult to make the case for change toward conscious, collaborative leadership. However, there are statistical indicators that demonstrate that this brand of leadership delivers measurable performance results. There are defined stages to our growth that validate and show us the cognitive path forward.

THE STAGES OF ADULT DEVELOPMENT

Much of today's understanding of adult development was

researched and authored by Robert Kegan, an American developmental psychologist with a forty-year career as a professor of adult learning and development at Harvard's Graduate School of Education. He and Lisa Lahey, also of the Harvard Graduate School of Education, made a breakthrough discovery on the hidden behavioral dynamic called the "Immunity to Change." My interest was piqued in reading their book of the same name, which featured research into the same wildland firefighting organizations with whom I worked. When a friend invited me to her office to observe the kickoff of her latest leadership development program, I found myself face-to-face with the co-founder of Kegan and Lahey's consulting practice.

Our worlds and work were colliding.

Leadership development of any kind needs to deliver results. Even though there are innumerable intangible benefits from any personal growth work, that is not enough to compel individuals and organizations to invest in it. Part of why I am drawn to adult development research is that it gives a framework that can be practically applied with measurable outcomes. Even the greatest of skeptics find it easy to understand and appreciate the value it provides.

The adult development framework features five stages of growth:[23]

- **Stage 1:** Impulsive mind (early childhood)
- **Stage 2:** Imperial mind (adolescence, 6 percent of adults)
- **Stage 3:** Socialized mind (58 percent of adults)
- **Stage 4:** Self-authoring mind (35 percent of adults)

---

23 Robert Kegan and Lisa Laskow Lahey, *Immunity to Change: How to Overcome It and Unlock Potential in Yourself and Your Organization* (Boston: Harvard Business Press, 2009).

- **Stage 5:** Self-transforming mind (1 percent of adults)

Each of us has the ability to progress through all stages. Our ability to grow is dependent on how we internalize and learn from the experiences that we have. Not only that, but we are able to design experiences that help advance our mental and emotional complexity. We don't have to wait for the right experience to come along to foster our development. We can create it.

The majority of adults spend their lives in the socialized and self-authoring minds. We will focus our discussion here. The self-transforming mind represents less than 1 percent of the adult population. It's leadership of the highest order, defined by the ability to "see beyond themselves, others, and systems of which they are a part to form an understanding of how all people and systems interconnect."[24] As we progress toward this fifth stage, we become more adaptive in our approaches, more conscious in our mindsets.

THE SOCIALIZED MIND

We spend a significant portion of our adult life in the socialized mind. It's during this stage that we build our sense of identity, importance, and security. We are shaped by the definitions and expectations of our personal environment. The norms of our family, social groups, religion, politics, and organizational cultures affect our perception of the world. By learning the "rules of the game" we are able to garner success and establish our role in

---

24   Robert Kegan, "What 'Form' Transforms? A Constructive-Developmental Approach to Transformative Learning," in *Learning as Transformation: Critical Perspectives on a Theory in Progress*, ed. Jack Mezirow (San Francisco: Jossey-Bass, 2000), https://eric.ed.gov/?id=ED448301.

society. Whether a stay-at-home parent or a CEO, our identity is tied to what we do, how well we do it, and the acceptance of others. At this stage, it's difficult for us to see that our goals and behaviors are driven by our environment.

Teams, organizations, and collaborations that operate from a socialized mind will tend toward groupthink. In an effort to avoid conflict, a group of socialized minds will less likely challenge an idea even if they don't believe it will be successful. Next time you are in a team setting, pay attention to the dynamics of the socialized mind at play. You'll see how highly attuned we are to verbal cues, intonation of voice, and body language. It's easy to spot impatience or frustration without a single word being spoken. Notice how quickly the individual or group moves to resolve it even if it's not addressed directly.

THE SELF-AUTHORING MIND

The self-authoring mind is the major transition in life. It's in this stage that we operate with acute attention to vision. We begin to "break the rules" of societal expectations, but differently than we did in our teenage years. We are driven by a sense of purpose and authentic expression, not an egoic desire to buck authority. We accept the very real truth that by following this path, we will disappoint people and our attempts may fail. Our position in society matters less than our ability to create a meaningful life. We want this for others too and foster its growth in them. In this way, we redefine power as something that is shared and not tied to hierarchy.

Two dominant characteristics of teams, organizations, and collaborations that operate from a self-authoring mind are transparency and focus. They are free from the fear of upsetting others, trust their and others' views are in service of creating shared value, and are willing to challenge their own beliefs and assumptions (or to have them be challenged by others). With this freedom comes the ability to focus on that which is most essential, strategic, and important. The result is a high-performing team that navigates the roles of leadership and followership intuitively. Thus, leadership becomes situational and not positionally predefined. Even the act of followership becomes a demonstration of leadership in this context.

MOVING FROM THE SOCIALIZED TO SELF-AUTHORING MIND

Only 25 percent of adults in our culture complete the full journey from socialized to self-authoring.[25] Carl Jung first popularized this transition as one across the "two halves of life." These two halves don't map to a chronological age. Nor is it possible to make a series of *grand jetés* to leap over the experience of the first half to get to the second half. This is not a highly choreo-graphed ballet or a race up the self-improvement staircase. The experiences and lessons of the socialized mind are necessary to build upon. As the Dalai Lama says, "Learn and obey the rules very well so you will know how to break them properly."

Growth in our mental complexity and consciousness is gradual. We progress, plateau, progress, plateau, and even regress at times. It's possible though to be quite young and operating from a self-authoring mind. Progress depends on active participation in our development. A baby learns to crawl before he can walk and walk before he can run. We would never say that crawling is *bad* and walking is *good*. They are simply different. Similarly,

---

25 Bob Anderson, "The Spirit of Leadership," Leadership Circle, March 2019, http://2y3l3p10hb5c1lkzte2wv2ks-wpengine.netdna-ssl.com/wp-content/uploads/2019/04/Spirit-of-Leadership-Whitepaper-V.2-MAR2019.pdf.

it's important not to label our own development in this way. That is a dualistic way of thinking that can be dangerous. Each mindset has its own gifts and challenges, which was also true in our growth as children.

What's important to remember, is through growth we become more effective leaders and are able to handle the ever-increasing complexity of the world we live in. There is overwhelming evidence that effective leadership drives tangible, bottom-line results.

THE BUSINESS CASE FOR CONSCIOUS LEADERSHIP

The science behind consciousness and mindsets is solid but is still a relatively emerging field that hasn't been accepted fully in organizational and business practices. In 2011, I sought out tools that could quantify where leaders fall along the spectrum of adult development. I wanted more than a theoretical understanding of the concepts. I wanted to prove, to myself and my clients, the measurable difference that leaders operating from a higher consciousness could make in bottom-line results.

Bob Anderson, the founder of a global leadership development and assessment company, had created such a tool based on the long lineage of applied research into individual and organizational leadership. He worked with the foremost experts of the time to develop a 360-degree evaluation that, in essence, determines the degree to which a leader is working from a socialized or self-authoring mind. Additionally, it surfaces the key competencies, beliefs, and assumptions driving the effectiveness of the leader.

Here's what we know from twenty years of application of this tool with hundreds of thousands of leaders, as well as from nearly a century of statistically validated leadership studies that assisted in its development:

- **Self-authoring leaders create environments where people are highly committed and engaged.** Employees report 57 percent greater job satisfaction and commitment when working for the top 10 percent of leaders. And 80 percent of employees "think about quitting" their jobs when reporting to the bottom 10 percent of leaders versus 4 percent who "think about quitting" if they report to leaders in the top 10 percent.[26]
- **Self-authoring leaders are more productive, especially in high-complexity situations.** When looking at the productivity of people doing the exact same work, the top 1 percent of leaders in a medium-complexity job were 85 percent more productive than the person in the fiftieth percentile. In high-complexity jobs, the top 1 percent was 127 percent more productive than the person in the fiftieth percentile.[27]
- **Self-authoring leaders maximize the results of their financial investments.** Less than 37 percent of employees who reported to the bottom 10 percent of leaders were satisfied with their pay. Compare that to the 60 percent who were satisfied with their pay in organizations led by the top 10 percent of leaders. What's more, the organizations led by

26 Jack Zenger and Joe Folkman, "How Extraordinary Leaders Double Profits: Why Excellent Leadership Deserves Your Attention," Zenger-Folkman, 2014. https://zengerfolkman.com/wp-content/uploads/2019/04/How-Extraordinary-Leaders-Double-Profits-LRC.pdf.

27 John Hunter et al., "Individual Differences in Output Variability as a Function of Job Complexity," *Journal of Applied Psychology* 75, no. 1 (1990): 28–42. https://doi.org/10.1037/0021-9010.75.1.28.

the top 10 percent of leaders did not pay their employees more than those in the bottom 10 percent.[28]

- **Self-authoring leaders deliver improved net outcomes, including profitability.** Commitment, engagement, wise use of financial resources, and productivity all contribute to the core mission and deliverables of any organization. An example of this is demonstrated by a study that shows the correlation between these elements and sales growth. In 2014, the Mexican economy struggled due to political problems and lower-than-expected growth. A retail store chain used the assessment I've described to address profitability. The results were clear. Leaders in the bottom 10 percent were only able to achieve a 0.7 percent profitability over the course of a year. The top 10 percent of leaders showed a 7.4 percent improvement.[29]

As a certified practitioner of this assessment for individuals and teams, I have seen the impact of this work firsthand. I have also seen that the number one reason these results aren't sustained is when the assessment is viewed as a one-off, interesting learning experience rather than a platform for continued growth. In fact, 87 percent of what a person learns from a leadership intervention like this assessment is forgotten within thirty days without follow-up.[30]

I can't emphasize enough that leadership is a long-term commitment. It must be practiced to achieve mastery. Through my twenty years of education, training, and experience, I have been able to distill all of this down into four *specific* practices.

---

28 Zenger and Folkman, "How Extraordinary Leaders Double Profits."

29 Ibid.

30 Neil Rackham, *SPIN Selling* (New York: McGraw-Hill Education, 1988).

Together, they form a collaborative leadership model that unlocks the power of relationship to create change. This model is the heart of my work as consultant, facilitator, and executive coach. When you integrate these practices into your life, your work, and your collaborative efforts, you will see results.

If you're feeling overwhelmed, remember that you are not starting from ground zero. You are already on the path of development. This model will serve to redirect, refine, and increase your effectiveness. And effectiveness matters. When it comes to performance measures, 37 percent of accomplishments are achieved through leadership effectiveness.[31]

What would be possible if we were able to enlist 37 percent more businesses in sustainability initiatives? Or if we were able to create a 37 percent reduction in carbon emissions? Or even if 37 percent more organizations were working together to solve the environmental crisis? Think how quickly we could scale our solutions.

Those 37 percent gains are immediately accessible to us. They're contained within and waiting to be unleashed. And just as certainly, our environmental and social challenges will outpace us if we don't act to harness the power of collaborative leadership. The four practices that span the next part of the book will not only teach you how to harness this power but to put it all together inside a framework that leads to collective action.

---

31 Bob Anderson, "The Leadership Circle® and Organizational Performance," https://2y3l3p10hb5c1lkzte2wv2ks-wpengine.netdna-ssl.com/wp-content/uploads/2018/03/The-Leadership-Circle-and-Organizational-Performance.pdf.

Part Two

THE FOUR PRACTICES OF COLLABORATIVE LEADERSHIP

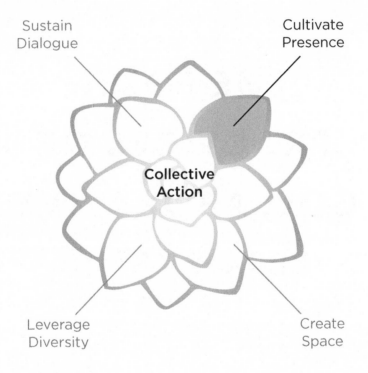

Sustain
Dialogue

Cultivate
Presence

Collective
Action

Leverage
Diversity

Create
Space

Chapter Three

CULTIVATE PRESENCE

The quieter you become, the more you can hear.

—BABA RAM DASS, AUTHOR OF *Be Here Now*

We can't understand what is happening to 'something' if we aren't looking. But nothing is going to happen to that 'something' if we don't look deeply. That is why so many things with incredible potential go unnoticed. Nobody bothers to look.

—ALEJANDRO GONZALEZ INARRITU, DIRECTOR OF
21 Grams, The Revenant, AND OTHER FILMS

I recently attended a meditation course with Jack Kornfield, who is trained as a Buddhist monk and credited as one of the key teachers to introduce mindfulness practices to the West.

He began the course in this way:

> There is a story of a famous biologist, George Schaller, whose work was carried on by Dian Fossey and portrayed in the movie *Gorillas in the Mist*.
>
> When he came back from studying the silverback gorillas in their native habitat, his research exposed relationships between their family structures and communities that no one had ever seen before.
>
> He later presented his findings at a large conference of biologists. At the end of his talk, someone raised their hand to ask, "Dr. Schaller, we've been studying gorillas in the scientific community for generations. You have so much more information than we've ever been able to discover. How did you do this?"
>
> His response was, "It's simple. I didn't carry a gun."

The generations of biologists that had studied the gorillas before Schaller had always carried elephant guns with them as a form of protection. The choice that Schaller made not to carry a gun seems obvious in hindsight. He was aware of the defensive posture that a weapon in his hands would create for the gorillas. He understood that it would prevent any chance to form the open relationship that was necessary to develop new understanding of their behaviors and social structure.

Kornfield further explained, "Schaller chose to come into the gorillas' presence respectfully, eyes downcast, and with a great sense of care."

This story is a powerful illustration of what you will learn in this chapter: leadership is built on a strong foundation of purpose, awareness, and receptivity to the present moment or, in a single word, flow. I bring in this example from the natural world to remind you that these are qualities that are innate to us. In our intellectual and professional pursuits, it's sometimes easy to lose sight of the fact that we are hardwired for connection. The story of Schaller and the gorillas reminds us that presence has the potential to heighten relationships and unlock new discoveries.

To cultivate presence means you become ever more capable of entering a state of flow to create positive outcomes. Although there are actions you must take to cultivate presence, this first leadership practice is less about what you *do* and more an expression of how you approach any given moment. In other words, leadership begins with an authentic state of *being* that is grounded in presence. It's through presence that we expand the possibilities for what we can create collectively.

THE EXPERIENCE OF PRESENCE

I want to invite you to experience the practice of cultivating presence for yourself, right here and now. Take a moment to shut down all of the distractions around you. Find a quiet place to be. Take a few deep breaths. Let yourself sit with ease and alertness. Settle in for just a few moments before you continue reading.

Now, think of a time when you felt deeply connected to the natural world. This memory may have taken place as a child or, perhaps, more recently. If you need to, close your eyes so that you can see it clearly. Don't just observe it from the outside, but step into that moment once again. Be part of it as though you were there for the first time. Notice the colors that you see, the sounds you hear, the smells that arise. Revisit the feel of the air and the taste of the season. Bring to life anyone that may have been part of this memory too.

Recall all that you can as you let yourself sit with this experience that is uniquely yours. Expand your awareness to include internal physical sensation. Where do you feel this memory most strongly? Does it strike a chord in your heart? Can you feel your feet planted solidly on the ground? Is there a rush of energy in your arms?

Finally, notice whatever emotions might be there too. You might feel calm or delight, melancholy or joy, curiosity or peace. You might not feel anything in particular. You can notice that too. Linger here, perhaps just past a point that feels comfortable. When you're ready, bring your attention back to the present moment and your surroundings.

As your attention returns to the words on this page, what stands out to you? What is the impact of the reflective pause? What new awareness do you have about the significance of that memory that you didn't initially recall?

Now consider the experience in the context of the whole of your life and work. What does it tell you about what you value? Who you are at your core? How does it connect you to your career, your passions, your work in collaborative leadership spaces, or in reading this book today?

I often begin work with clients using this type of exercise.[32] To strengthen collaborative leadership in teams, I take it one step further by asking them to share their experiences with one another. There is an immediate shift that happens through this process. By connecting first to themselves and then to one another, there is heightened openness.

The exercise reminds them of what drives them as people, not just as professionals. Bridges of understanding begin to form, including between those who were complete strangers minutes before. There is a palpable sense of vitality in the room after this exercise. It breathes life into everyone.

Most importantly, by bringing the group into a state of presence, an identity begins to take shape. As each person shares their story in a larger group, there is a natural tendency to weave together the threads that are common and celebrate the uniqueness of those that are not. A new narrative emerges. It's one that will form the foundation for later alignment around vision, goals, and strategy. It connects the *me* to the *we*, which is a muscle that we need to build in support of the other collaborative leadership practices.

THE SIMPLICITY OF PRACTICE

Have you ever initiated a meeting or professional gathering in this way? My guess is likely not. Cultivating presence has a meditative quality to it. It can feel awkward and vulnerable, especially if you don't habitually engage in individual presence-based practices like meditation.

---

32 At the end of this silent reflection, I give my clients time to write about their experience. You might take the opportunity to do that too, using the questions I ask of them as a guide. This is an actionable step you can take to cultivate presence.

For some it feels "too soft," "touchy-feely," "completely irrele-vant," or "like a waste of time" when there is "so much to get done." If you find yourself feeling similarly, I understand. I have heard these exact sentiments expressed to me before. And yet I have witnessed over and over again the quality of interaction rise when we take the time to cultivate presence. The invest-ment of time required to arrive with presence ultimately leads to better, longer-lasting results.

The practice of cultivating presence doesn't have to be a soul search every time. In fact, when we simplify the practice, we become more likely to engage with it. The more that we engage with this or any of the other leadership practices in the whole of our lives, the more adept we become at using them collab-oratively. We must learn to speak a new leadership language. And, like any language, it takes deliberate practice to become truly fluent.

As I write this, I am traveling through Spain. It's taken almost the whole week to get in the groove of speaking another lan-guage. I once called myself fluent, but I've stumbled these last seven days. It wasn't until I started speaking Spanish, not only with others but also internally with *myself*, that my brain was able to break through the feeling of incompetence and relax into feeling at ease with my words. To ensure that my next trip doesn't feel like a language crash-course, I bought a few books written in Spanish. I've purposefully selected books that aren't extraordinarily complicated. I'll take them home to practice on my own so that, later, I will be better prepared to navigate my travels abroad and build relationships with the people I meet.

We can become relatively fluent in presence by cultivating it on our own. But when a group practices presence together, it becomes a shared language that they can drop into together with ease. This practice *can* be simple. Sometimes, all it takes is a single question to connect a group of people to themselves as individuals and to one another in the group: What do you need to leave behind that will allow you to be present for our time together?

When I pose this question to a group, I ask for a short, one-sentence response. The purpose is to offer a pause for reflection. All of us always have something running in the background—a sick child, a busy afternoon, a vacation that is coming. These things pull our emotions and attention in different directions. We sacrifice the power of our presence. Even if what we are distracted by is positive, we're not in the moment. To come into presence fully means to let go of everything except what's in front of us.

The reflective pause inherent in a simple question like this causes us to see clearly the spectrum of things that have us distracted. Our modern lives keep us operating on overload. In this environment, our minds aren't much different than computers with multiple windows open at once. We bounce from one thing to the next with the hope that something hasn't spiraled out of control while our attention was elsewhere. We limit our headway on the thing that we originally sat down to do.

Research shows that our brains cannot process two cognitive tasks at once. As an example, texting while driving is the equivalent of driving with a blood-alcohol level three times the legal limit.[33] I say this with an edge of humor grounded in reality:

---

33   "Mobile Phone Use: A Growing Problem of Driver Distraction," World Health Organization, February 14, 2011, https://www.who.int/publications/i/item/mobile-phone-use-a-growing-problem-of-driver-distraction.

the future of our planet deserves thoughtful decision-making made by unimpaired people. Yet we are challenged more and more every day to manage our schedules, technology, and commitments. We glorify busyness as a sign of progress. How much greater might our impact be if we were to approach our most complex challenges with the focus that presence provides?

The verbal articulation of the multiple things on our mind is one way to shortcut distraction. Neuroscience tells us that stating a problem out loud can release its hold on our attention and worry.[34] It calms the brain and body simultaneously. It's almost as if you are saying to yourself and neurocircuitry, "Okay, thoughts. I know that you're stressed about that, but I promise you that I'll give it attention later. For now, I have to focus on this." By no means does this make the child get better, the afternoon be lighter, or shorten the time between you and your vacation. But it can bring you back to the moment and cue yourself to put it aside. It has the added benefit that others know how you're arriving to the conversation, which will enhance the leadership practice of dialogue that we'll explore later.

Try it for yourself. Take a pause. Scan your mind for all of the mental computer windows you have open. What needs to be closed so that you can focus on the words on the page? One by one, say *out loud* the issues, tasks, or worries that occupy your mental space. Tell yourself that you will return to those thoughts later. See how it shifts your quality of attention.

---

34 University of California, Los Angeles, "Putting Feelings into Words Produces Therapeutic Effects in the Brain," *ScienceDaily*, June 22, 2007, https://www.sciencedaily.com/releases/2007/06/070622090727.htm.

A ROAD MAP TO PRESENCE

We live in a time where words like *presence* and *mindfulness* have made their way into mainstream conversation. Yet, for most people, what those words mean and how to apply them practically within a professional setting isn't quite clear. I've given you two examples of how I bring presence into collaborative environments: one with a deeper meditative practice and one with a simple question. But even these two approaches seem vastly different and unlikely to be applicable to every situation. In this way, presence begins to feel like a kaleidoscope of concepts that keeps shifting without ever forming a discernable pattern.

What's more, we see these concepts gaining ground in highly credible organizations but never quite in the same way. Military forces throughout the world teach meditation as a core part of their strategy.[35] (Apparently, as George Schaller's story demonstrates, even those who *do* carry guns know the difference presence can make.) Google offers a mindful leadership course to the public that was once only available to its employees. And UN humanitarian workers use presence as a way to manage stress when working in some of the most dangerous areas of the world.[36]

"Ecological mindfulness" is gaining ground too. Still in its infancy, research shows that there is a relationship between mindfulness and sustainability. In examining the impact of mindfulness related to climate change and risk reduction, studies show that there is a positive influence on deliberate, flexible,

---

35   Matt Richtel, "The Latest in Military Strategy: Mindfulness" *New York Times*, April 5, 2019, https://www.nytimes.com/2019/04/05/health/military-mindfulness-training.html.

36   Melissa Locker, "Lululemon Is Helping the UN's Humanitarian Aid Workers Take Care of Themselves," *Fast Company*, October 8, 2019, https://www.fastcompany.com/90414681/lululemon-is-helping-the-uns-humanitarian-aid-workers-take-care-of-themselves.

and adaptive responses, particularly in postdisaster scenarios.[37] Other studies show the impact of mindfulness on increasing an individual's ability to balance macro and micro perspectives.[38] This capability is extremely important in a world with chronic global environmental challenges and acute local symptoms.

These are powerful testaments to the importance of presence-based practices. They have validated their functional utility and catalyzed organizations of all sizes and sectors to move in similar directions. But without a one-size-fits-all definition of how to apply these practices in a meaningful way, we see organizations establishing programs or initiatives in the hopes that they will have a long-standing impact. Employees might be led through a meditation by their wellness team, but these types of activities rarely become part of everyday work culture.

Each of us holds in our mind's eye different concepts about what it might take to cultivate presence as part of our personal and professional lives. We step cautiously, unsure if it brings any value.

- "Will I have to start doing yoga?"
- "Are they going to make me meditate?"
- "Only *they* do that kind of thing."

These are deeply ingrained beliefs, assumptions, and projected images around what it means to practice presence. Right or wrong, they influence how (or whether) we choose to develop mastery of it. There isn't one pathway to presence. But there are

---

37 Christine Wamsler et al., "Mindfulness in Sustainability Science, Practice, and Teaching." *Sustainability Science* 13, no. 1 (April 5, 2017): 143–62. https://doi.org/10.1007/s11625-017-0428-2.

38 Ibid.

three fundamental concepts that will help you, your team, your organization, and your collaborations engage in presence-based approaches in practical ways.

Presence is often described as paying attention in a particular way: on purpose, in the present moment, and nonjudgmentally. We'll use this definition to guide how to cultivate presence in your individual and collaborative leadership work. I simplify this definition into three concrete steps: defining purpose, expanding awareness, and finding flow.

PURPOSE: DEFINE WHAT MATTERS MOST

Presence originates from purpose. Whether we are gathering around a conference table to discuss complex environmental issues or around the dinner table to share a meal with our family, defining what matters most to us in that moment is what creates impact. Every moment of every day, we have the opportunity to cultivate presence by setting mindful intentions for our interactions.

Purpose can sometimes feel overwhelming to define. This is especially true in collaborative environments with an all-encompassing vision of a more sustainable planetary future. The power of cultivating presence as a leadership practice is that it allows us to move toward that vision step by step, moment by moment. Defining too big of a purpose becomes aspirational and unwieldy. Too small of a purpose becomes uninspiring and lacks direction. Both approaches, whether too big or too small, stagnate forward movement or lead toward inauthentic action. It's when we correctly size our purpose to the present moment that we become capable of aligning our diverse perspectives and needs so that we can take meaningful action today.

When designing collaborative engagements, there are two questions that I use to guide my clients toward a deeper understanding of purpose:

- What is the compelling reason for being here *today?*
- What is the compelling reason for doing this work *right now?*

Write these questions down. Put them in your back pocket. Carry them with you.

Creating systems-level change is a massive undertaking with many contingencies and shifting variables. If you, like my clients, are working toward goals that are decades in the future, these are questions that will help you to distill your thinking. That isn't to say that you develop tunnel vision or abandon your larger goal. To the contrary, these questions offer you the chance to quiet the noise, excitement, and anxiety that too much possibility creates. It's in this silence that you can tune in to a deeper wisdom of the most essential elements of your work.

A few years ago, a founder of a social enterprise hired me to facilitate a strategic plan progress review with his board of directors. In preparation for the meeting, his staff pulled together accomplishment reports on each area of the plan. By all accounts, the quantitative and qualitative results were impressive. The enterprise had met or exceeded all of its annual objectives. The success stories that they told were compelling. And they were well-positioned financially.

It would have been a quick win to celebrate the accomplishments, sign off on the next year's action plan, and call it a day. But in our discussions leading up to the meeting, the founder challenged himself to dig a little deeper. Beyond what the numbers demonstrated, he sensed that there was something missing. As we talked about the purpose of the progress review meeting, I asked him what he felt was the most important reason for gathering together this group of advisors at this moment of heightened success.

His response provides insight into the importance of defining what matters:

> Laura, this company is on a steady growth path. We're set to hit our five-year targets. I have incredible support from investors and the board. My employees are happy and excited to come to work. All of us are 100 percent committed to the vision and mission of this company. We believe in the impact that it will make.
>
> But I think we could accomplish more and in more significant ways with less near-term growth. If we took a step back and made a strategic investment of resources into something that may not be realized for some years to come, we would be better off in the end.
>
> I may be crazy to say that. I am terrified to share this with the Board. But this is the most meaningful conversation I could have about the direction we take next. Our meeting is an opportunity to do that.

In this single reflection, he shifted the purpose of the board meeting from a perfunctory event to one with relevant, meaningful focus. The purpose wasn't too big in that he wasn't trying to upend the goals of the company or the progress that had been made thus far. And it wasn't too small in that he wasn't focused on implementing the plan that was already in place. Instead, the purpose of the meeting became more strategic and asked the question, "What would it look like if we were to take a slower growth path?" It was this question that guided the design of the meeting and the dialogue that took place there.

When we are explicit about defining and communicating our purpose, we maximize our outcomes. No matter what the decision was that he and the board made that day, it created intention that pointed everyone's attention toward exploring the best path forward.

AWARENESS: EXPAND ATTENTION

Attention follows intention. Once we are clear on our purpose or intention for any given moment, we continue to cultivate presence through an ever-expanding awareness of the context that surrounds it.

As collaborative leaders, presence means having a focus for our work while maintaining a more global awareness of the factors influencing it and—perhaps, more importantly—us. That kind of global awareness requires a fluid ability to change the lens between direct, soft, and expansive ways of paying attention. Without this ability, we risk becoming so attached to a specific outcome that we miss critical details that could enhance or limit our effectiveness.

There is a famous study that was conducted in the late nineties on selective attention. The study demonstrates that hyperfocus on a particular task can create blindness to new stimuli. Study participants are asked to watch a video of people passing basketballs. Half of the people in the video are wearing white. Half are wearing black. The researchers ask the study participants to count how many times the people in white pass the basketball to each other while ignoring the people in black. About midway through the video, someone dressed in a black gorilla suit passes through the scene thumping his chest. While you may think that something so blatant would be impossible to miss, consider this: about 50 percent of study participants failed to notice the gorilla.[39]

Our world's environmental challenges are a lot more difficult to observe than what takes place in this study's video. They are interwoven with social, political, and economic factors. There are visible and invisible forces at play, but the cause and effect it is not always clear. And the threats we face are more imposing than a man in a gorilla suit. We must learn to draw our collective attention to one part of the intricate web of issues, but not so selectively that we aren't open to new information, emerging patterns, or shifts in our thoughts, emotions, or beliefs.

Purpose helps us to focus our attention, and the collaborative nature of our work provides a buffer to ensure we don't become unintentionally blind to other factors. But external awareness is only one part of the equation. We also need to be attuned to what is happening within so that we can access more information. The most powerful tool that we can use to broaden our internal awareness in this way is our body.

Here's a quick evolutionary biology lesson.

Our prefrontal cortex is responsible for complex thought. It has evolved with a highly specialized function of external attention. Research shows that older and more buried parts of our brain—

39   Daniel J. Simmons and Christopher F. Chabris, "Gorilla in Our Midst: Sustained Inattentional Blindness for Dynamic Events," *Perception* 28, no. 9 (1999): 1059–1074, DOI: 10.1068/p281059.

like the insula and posterior cingulate cortex—are specialized in observing our internal landscape.[40] Most of us prioritize external attention, or *exteroceptive attention*, focusing our thoughts on things and people outside of us. We only tend to turn inwardly when our feelings are intense: a spark of anger in response to getting cut off in traffic or the involuntary blush of warmth when we feel attraction. Yet there is significant evidence that training ourselves to tap into our body's wisdom habitually—our *interoceptive attention*—leads to emotional states of well-being, decreased stress, and enhanced decision-making.

Think of the common phrases that we use: "My mind was racing," "I just needed to get out of my head," or "I can't shut off my brain." Too much exteroceptive focus will create this kind of overwhelm. It's when we get back into our bodies that we return to a calmer, more centered, clearheaded space. When I get too cognitively focused, I know it's time to head out the door for a run and shake loose the cobwebs. It's also why practices like meditation and yoga are so useful. They use the breath to create a connection between *exteroceptive* and *interoceptive* attention. A phenomenon many people often cite is the experience of having a lucid download of thoughts while showering. (This is common enough that there are whiteboards specifically made for the shower.)

Where does all of this ultimately lead us? We can expand our attention through heightened mind-body awareness. Recall the exercise I led you through at the beginning of this chapter. There was a point at which I asked you to connect with the physical sensation that your memory created. You can do something similar when those moments of intense focus on

---

40   Norman A. S. Farb, Zindel V. Segal, and Adam K. Anderson, "Attentional Modulation of Primary Interoceptive and Exteroceptive Cortices," *Cerebral Cortex* 23, no. 1 (January 19, 2012): 114–126. https://doi.org/10.1093/cercor/bhr385.

a problem feel restrictive or unproductive. Stop to do a body check. Notice where your body is in space. Notice where you're holding (or not holding) tension. Notice whether your breath is shallow and quick or deep and calm. Take a deep breath. Step away for a walk outside. And then, from there, notice how you can see the challenge in front of you anew.

I advocated earlier that cultivating presence can be simple. But it does require that we drop the bias that the only way to *know* is through our thoughts. We become more attuned when we strike the balance between an external focus on the issue before us and rely on internal emotional awareness that creates the ability to see it within a holistic context.

FLOW: FIND MEANING IN EACH MOMENT

From here, we are able to explore a range of solutions without attachment to one idea or solution being the *right* one. If we actively engage purpose and awareness, we can take the next step of finding meaning in each moment. In positive psychology, this is known as a flow state or "being in the zone." It's the place where we are fully immersed in our experience and its unfolding process.

One of the biggest hurdles that leaders face is embracing the ever-changing nature that adaptive, systems-level challenges present. As we explored in chapter 2, adaptive challenges require us to be in a state of constant experimentation as we learn our way to innovative solutions. The engagement of flow helps overcome the inner conflict that naturally arises when something difficult stretches us in ways we have not yet experienced. Flow transforms the anxiety of situations into a healthy creative tension. It's in that creative tension that we find joy and meaning in the process of closing the gap between our current reality and our future vision.

Where I often see leaders get wrapped around the axle is that they are constantly measuring the gap between where they are and where they want to be. Or they want to close it as quickly as possible. Their minds are always future-pacing. They judge the present moment as valuable only insofar as it escalates their progress toward a goal. In short, their judgment blocks them from deriving any pleasure in the present moment. Leadership feels like a struggle. Reaching their goal feels like striving for something that is constantly out of reach.

It's within our power to shift this experience. When we consciously choose to find meaning in the present moment, we open ourselves up to new definitions of success. We change our minds. In his book *Flow*, Mihaly Csikszentmihalyi describes the freedom that this can provide:

> To the extent that a glamorous ad makes us salivate for the product sold or that a frown from the boss spoils the day, we are not free to determine the content of experience. Since what we experience is reality, as far as we are concerned, we can transform reality to the extent that we influence what happens in consciousness and thus free ourselves from the threats and blandishments of the outside world.

> "Men are not afraid of things, but of how they view them," said Epictetus a long time ago. And the great emperor Marcus Aurelius wrote: "If you are pained by external things, it's not that they disturb you, but your own judgment of them. And it's in your power to wipe out that judgment now."[41]

---

41   Mihaly Csikszentmihalyi, *Flow* (New York: Harper Collins, 1990), 19.

Instead of our thoughts constantly tumbling forward, flow allows us to train our minds to the here and now. Instead of fixating on what's not happening, flow allows us to participate with curiosity. Instead of digging in on what we don't like, flow allows us to use our gifts and strengths to create something new. It's possible to do this with any task, but it can become a delight when we are committed fully to a worthy cause.

There is always a moment in every collaborative engagement when I see the lightbulbs go off on what it means to be in flow. This is the moment when individuals come together as a team. It's also the moment when participants see the leadership role that they play. There are two factors that are usually at play when this happens:

1. A novel idea emerges from within the group that taps into personal and collective purpose.
2. There is a recognition that the process of collaboration leverages and amplifies the strengths each individual brings. No one person can implement the idea alone. And everyone has to be all in.

As an outside observer and guide of the collaborative process, to me, it looks like instant cohesion. Like a disappearing background in a movie scene, I witness the external distractions fall away. The resistance to the process dissipates. While the ultimate goal is still important, it's not primary anymore. Instead there is a quality in the room of "everyone is here" for what's going on today—together, present, and accounted for.

This is where magic begins to happen. But where does the spark of an idea come from? How do you create the conditions for powerful ideas that evoke change? Doing the work of defining purpose and expanding awareness are the first steps. Dropping attachments to outcomes, limiting our judgments of the work at hand, and finding meaning in the moment come next. In this way, we begin to recognize that presence is a cornerstone of action.

But even greater answers lay in the next leadership practice, as we begin to create space for collaboration to occur.

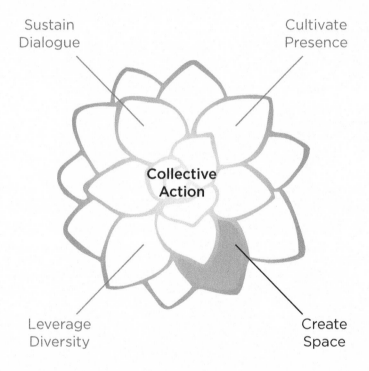

Sustain
Dialogue

Cultivate
Presence

**Collective
Action**

Leverage
Diversity

Create
Space

Chapter Four

CREATE SPACE

Between stimulus and response there is a space. In that space is the power to choose our response. In our response lies our growth and freedom.

—VICTOR E. FRANKL, AUSTRIAN NEUROLOGIST
AND HOLOCAUST SURVIVOR

Opportunity Collaboration (OC) is a global network of leaders dedicated to building sustainable solutions to poverty and injustice. Every year, they host an event that invites people from around the world, in multiple sectors, and a range of disciplines with a vested interest in these topics. Attendees run the gamut from grant makers to impact investors, from corporations to academia, from government to nonprofits, and from social entrepreneurs to journalists. The purpose of this "unconference" (as they like to call it) is to create the kinds of connections that lead to new ideas, unexpected partnerships, and amplified impact.

In 2012, I was invited to attend as a facilitator of daily round-table discussions. These sessions were held each morning as a way to create connection between participants on global poverty themes they all cared about. I used many of the presence-based practices discussed in the last chapter to ground my cohort into a deeper intention for their day. But there was something else at play that would help them put that intention into action: the space that surrounded them.

We were at a Club Med in Ixtapa, Mexico. Yes, I said Club Med. And I do mean the all-inclusive resort with a series of reputations over the years, none of which relate to poverty alleviation.

This seemed to me like a strange location for OC to choose. That is, until I arrived and saw how it perfectly supported the summit's purpose. The entire facility was dedicated to the event. Attending the event meant that you were a guest of the resort, and all guests of the resort were part of the event. For five days, everyone you crossed paths with was guaranteed to share similar values. Everyone you met had a desire to create real impact through their work, *and* they were doing it.

The all-inclusive nature of the resort accomplished something important. It leveled privilege and power dynamics. That meant that impact investors with significant capital and nonprofit leaders operating in developing countries ate the same meals in the same restaurants, had access to the same amenities, and stayed in the same type of room. The conference registration fee varied for attendees depending on income level to ensure diverse participation was possible.

Once you arrived, every detail was taken care of for you—no matter who you were, where you came from, or how much you had. Name tags were just that: names only. If you wanted to know more about someone, you had to ask. Mailboxes were set up for each attendee to courier messages between sessions. It was an ingenious way to get an introduction you might otherwise be hesitant to ask for. There were no business suits. Relaxing in a hammock was a perfectly acceptable way to collaborate. The sea breeze, the sound of the waves rolling into the shore, and the lush gardens were the backdrop for conversations that led to new solutions. And with everything and everyone at ease, new ideas flowed freely.

Years later, OC continues to host their event at Club Meds and has since expanded to multiple geographies. I asked Topher Wilkins, executive director of OC, to weigh in on what he thought made the space so special. He echoed much of what I have shared here but offered a few more insights:

> When it comes to leaders collaborating, the space provides unprecedented opportunity for people to interact with each other and maximize the depth and breadth of relationship building. The space ensures the same group of people are seeing each other over and over.

The space also levels the playing field. It's not like funders get to reserve a suite at the Ritz while nonprofit leaders have to watch their budget during the week. No one pays for anything while we're there. Gone are the power dynamics of someone pulling out their Amex Black card and saying, "This dinner is on me." In fact, the most common joke at OC is, "I'll grab this round of drinks!" It's funny because there's an open bar the whole time we're there.

Furthermore, the space is designed to encourage attendees to step outside of their professional personas and their standard networking approach. Instead of the standard stoic, professional environment where the goal is to shuffle around as many business cards as possible, Club Med allows us to show up as our whole selves, personal, professional, and even parental. Delegates can bring their kids, spouses, or extended family members to enjoy the resort. They don't have to leave their personal lives behind to attend a professional event.

If you can get people to show up as whole, authentic human beings and be in a space where they can have raw, meaningful, vulnerable conversations, then you start to get to the heart of who we are and why we care about these issues. Once we have a foundation of trust, empathy, and whole-person shared experience, then we can build far more effective partnerships and collaborations in service of our collective impact mission.

My conversation with Wilkins underscored the premise of this leadership practice. It's not just the space that we operate in that's important, it's how the space gets used. OC takes this seriously. It's an essential part of their success. After all, they were able to strip away the pretense that is normally associated with all-inclusive resorts and transform it into a poverty alleviation think tank.

One of the most powerful moments that I had while attending OC was an afternoon of ocean swimming. The waves that day were some of the largest I've ever seen, but also quite gentle. It was like riding a very slow roller coaster. In true OC fashion, everyone in the water was meeting each other for the first time. I spent an hour talking to a woman from Malawi who ran an education nonprofit for girls. Now in her late sixties, she explained how profound it was to see the success of women who had come through her programs twenty years ago.

It was a *raw*, *meaningful*, and *vulnerable* conversation that might not have happened if it weren't for some playtime in the Pacific Ocean. I left knowing *who she is* and *why she cares*. As we got out of the water, a huge smile spread across her face: "That was so much fun. I've never seen the ocean before."

My heart melted.

Space is so much more than a meeting room or a venue. There are layers to it—both seen and unseen—that have the power to shift people and, in turn, outcomes. It matters how we invite someone into the space, how we leverage our physical environment, and how we shape a shared experience. While not every collaborative engagement will look like OC, it demonstrates that space is more than a detail and that it deserves your attention.

Creating space is an opportunity to understand the role that leaders play as hosts, inviting participation from all sides of an issue and creating an experience where every contribution matters.

THE INVITATION

When was the last time you were excited to receive an invitation to an event? Whether personal or professional, the invitation alone was meaningful. To be invited to this event carried weight or inspired delight. It was an invitation that gained your commitment to attend, almost instantly.

From the moment you received that invitation to the time that you said yes, a series of almost invisible steps occurred. These steps happen with every invitation we receive. Sometimes they happen quickly, sometimes slowly. First, you receive the invitation. Second, you notice that it exists. Third, you deliberate as to whether you want to dedicate your resources (time, money, attention) to attend. Fourth, you commit. Fifth, you prepare to attend.

There is an emotional journey that occurs from start to finish. What moves you from one step to the next happens internally. You're searching for the kind of resonance that would lead you to accept the invitation. You ask yourself:

- "How do I know that I am needed?"
- "What would I gain by attending? What would I lose by not?"
- "Who else is going? Who else would make it worth going?"
- "What value can I add to the event? What value does it bring to me?"

These are natural questions, whether the invitation is to a wedding, a meeting, or to partner in a collaboration. Even in those cases, where we feel obliged to attend, we still ask these questions of ourselves. They help us to discern our willingness and the mindset that we have going into it.

Think of the last time that you issued an invitation of your own:

- How did you help people understand the purpose of the event?
- How did you determine who would be invited?
- What did the invitation look like?
- What was the tone or energy behind it?
- How did you deliver it?
- What kind of follow-up did you do?
- What response did you get?

Creating a compelling invitation can be the difference between a lackluster engagement and one where people walk into the room enthused to get to work.

When a client works with me for the first time, it's not unusual that they have already started inviting people to collaborate. What that invitation often looks like is the definition of a problem statement or outcome stated as the meeting purpose, dates, times, and a location. This is sufficient for more traditional, well-understood gatherings for which people are accustomed to receiving invitations:

Come to my birthday party! We're going to an Atlanta Braves game on June 10th at 1 p.m. Food and drinks will be provided!

It's time for our quarterly strategy review. We'll meet in our staff conference room on Wednesday at 12 p.m. Be prepared to provide an update on your team's progress and recommendations for next quarter.

But remember, when we invite people to collaborate around the scale of environmental issues that we face, we are often defining, understanding, and solving adaptive challenges. This means we are inviting them to participate in something inherently difficult and uncertain. These factors make it easier to disengage, unless people are clear they have a role to play, feel that they can make a valuable contribution, and can find benefit in it for advancing their personal and organizational mission.

The space that the invitation creates is one in which a cocollaborator can respond with a powerful yes or no. The no is just as important as the yes. If the invitation is well crafted, it isn't a failure on your part to be persuasive enough. It means that you'll bring people to the table who are ready. Momentum will build from there, and people will opt in and out as the collaboration unfolds. A "no" can mean "not yet." A "maybe" can mean "help me to understand more."

You likely will not capture the time or attention of everyone you hope to engage. If you've been deliberate in your invitation, the right people will be in the room. They will be the ones who are clearest and most aligned with your purpose. They will help to deepen it. And they will open their networks, be your advocates, and expand the work.

CRAFTING THE INVITATION

There's bad news and good news. The bad news: I can't tell you what your invitation should look like. You will need to determine the best approach to move people from an internal space of consideration and into the physical space where collaboration will take place. This requires personalization and careful thought.

The good news: I can guide you through the principles that will help you shape your invitation. The process is outlined below in four steps that are meant to be done sequentially.

Purpose: Define the purpose of your collaborative gathering.

Ask yourself a simple but meaningful question: "What is the compelling reason for doing this work now?"

You'll notice that purpose shows up in both the previous chapter and this one. The question is even similar. This underscores how important it is to understand what is most important to you and why. Articulating the purpose as part of the invitation cues potential participants to connect with their own sense of purpose and presence. This is how they determine whether they will engage. Write a simple, well-defined purpose statement. This statement should provide a shared direction and intention for your work. Use the question about finding a compelling reason to zero in on a purpose that will motivate participation.

Outcomes: Determine the desired outcomes of your gathering.

To deliver on the promise of your meeting's purpose, it's important to decide up front what participants will leave the meeting with. These results can be tangible (like a report or strategy) or intangible (like increased trust). Use the questions below to identify the results that you want participants to experience in their head (or the domain of knowledge), heart (or the domain of relationships), and hands (or the domain of action).

- What do we hope the tangible and intangible results of our work will be?
- What new knowledge will be built?
- How will relationships be different?

- What action will be taken?

Stakeholders: Identify the stakeholders that are essential for success.

Before you start to list all of the people who you are already considering for an invitation, take the essential step of asking these questions:

- How will we sustain momentum?
- How will we make action happen?

Begin with a brainstorm of your answers to these questions. It may be helpful to think about these answers in the near term, midterm, and long term. This will help to ensure that you stay aligned with the meeting's purpose, which should be considerably smaller than the overarching purpose for the collaboration.

Once you have these answers, use them to identify a network of people who could influence the outcome of your work, whether allies or adversaries. The stakeholder map will help you to visualize the concentric circles of impact.

THE NETWORK OF PEOPLE WHO COULD INFLUENCE THE OUTCOME OF YOUR WORK
(WHETHER ALLIES OR ADVERSARIES)

PEOPLE WHO NEED TO KNOW
BUT ARE NOT ACTIVELY INVOLVED

PEOPLE TO
CONSULT

ESSENTIAL
PARTICIPANTS

CORE
TEAM

MEETING
PURPOSE

- Place your meeting's purpose in the center.
- Place the name of your core team in the first ring. These are the people that are most fully committed to and responsible for the engagement's success.
- On the second ring, place the names of individuals who are essential participants in the process but not part of the core team. These might be people whose expertise you need or whose political influence could sustain the work.
- On the third ring, place the names of people who you will consult with and keep closely informed about the process. They may not have decision-making authority, but not including them as invitees will diminish the work.
- Finally, on the fourth ring, place the names of people who will need to know about the meeting and its outcomes but don't necessarily need to be engaged.

Depending on the scope of your meeting's purpose, you will need to determine who from your network map needs to be invited. Organizing stakeholders in this way gives you a clear picture of who is connected to the work, how to best involve them, and what kind of invitation they might need.

Once you have completed these steps, *now* is the time to think about the invitation itself.

Invitation: Craft a clear and powerful invitation.

To craft a clear and powerful invitation, focus on the innermost rings of your stakeholder map. Consider what they might need to know in order to come open, excited, and ready to work. Begin by answering the following:

- What is the inspiring question that will bring people together?
- How will we invite people so that they know they are needed?
- What mediums will we use to invite people into the work of our physical space?
- Who do we need to engage in making the invitations?

The overarching invitation to all participants should focus on an inspiring question that draws people into the meeting's purpose. It could be future-oriented (e.g., What is possible if we succeed in our work together? Or how could collaborating with diverse partners help us to advance the goals of your organization?) It might also be needs-based (e.g., What is the cost of not acting now? What resources might others have that would help to amplify your work?)

With the overarching invitation in mind, it's important to think of personal invitations that are needed. These are one-to-one invitations that are done through phone calls or in-person meetings. Yes, this is an investment of time. Because of that, it's a step that is often skipped. The personal invitation with individuals helps them to connect more deeply with their own purpose and role. This is especially important for participants who may not know anyone else participating. Think about it, how often do you go to a party where you know no one except *maybe* the host? Asking other participants to reach out to these individuals helps to create a welcoming atmosphere where they know their participation is needed.

Solidify the Invitation

I walk my clients through purpose, outcomes, stakeholders, and invitation in the design of collaborative engagements. It gives them a structured approach to defining the high-level details of their gathering. With this in hand, I know how to design a process that maximizes participation and drives toward intended outcomes.

You'll notice I have mentioned *nothing* about the agenda yet. Ideally, all elements of the invitation would be in place before a conversation about the agenda and logistics begin. These elements help determine the best way to approach the length of the gathering, the place where it occurs, and the ways that participants need to be prepared in advance. However, we don't live in a perfect world. There are often constraints around the time and resources that you, as the convener, can commit or want to ask of your partners to commit.

In that case, it's extremely important to ensure the meeting's purpose isn't too ambitious to fit within those constraints. Do not risk losing continued engagement by setting expectations too high and not being able to deliver. At the same time, I challenge you to consider whether your limitations are, indeed, limitations. Are you assuming that people won't dedicate more time? Travel further? Invest more resources? And if so, is your invitation compelling enough?

Once you feel that your invitation is solid, it's time to consider the more traditionally thought-of physical space and the details of the agenda. There is a golden opportunity for leaders who understand the influence of both of these aspects of collaboration. The physical space and what happens within it are the driving force for the outcomes that will be created there.

THE CONTAINER

The boundaries of a watershed. The borders of state or nation. The lines that separate public land from private land. Even the doorways that lead us from one room to another or from indoors to outdoors. Every day, we cross over from place to place, some created by nature and some man-made. Each is a threshold that we pass through that gives us some felt sense of what the environment is designed to do and how we behave within it.

And there are invisible lines, too, between *you* and *me* and *we*. These lines originate from our culture, our race, our religion or spirituality (or lack thereof), our politics, our age, our gender identification, our education, our social class, our perspectives—which all lead to our experience of ourselves and others. We'll build on these further in the next chapter that focuses on diversity. But here too, it's important to call attention to it.

There is so much separation that it's no wonder collaboration is a challenge. We ask people to work through this separation when we invite them to collaborate. But little attention is paid to the way that space impacts our ability to do that. The leadership practice of creating space is an opportunity to create a *container* that is uniquely designed for the work of collaboration. It holds diverse perspectives and people together so that they can engage with one another in creative, strategic, and even challenging ways.

I use the word *container* to emphasize how multifaceted the concept of *space* is. It isn't just the four walls of a meeting room, but everything contained within it as well. Think of a vase. It can hold flowers with water, or it can be filled with jelly beans. The physical structure stays the same, but the utility and meaning of it changes. And not every container is built for the same thing. A woven basket wouldn't hold flowers with water very effectively, but it could easily transport any array of candy. The container we choose is just as important as what we put in it. Understanding this is critical to collaborative leadership.

Nature, too, can help us consider the importance of choosing the right container. Growing up in Arizona, my parents had a Southern live oak in the front yard. It was beautiful and distinct from the desert ecosystem that surrounded it. When I moved to the southeastern United States many years later, I came to understand how limited that tree was in its ability to flourish. Walking through Savannah, Georgia, the live oaks were easily four times its size. They lined the streets, creating majestic canopies, and were draped with Spanish moss. The right container created the right conditions for this tree to do the ecological "work" that it was meant to do.

When you learn the leadership practice of creating space, you take responsibility for the design of the container. You advocate for physical spaces that are supportive of collaborative work. These spaces will look and feel different than traditional meetings. You dedicate resources to building these containers, knowing that they break down the well-worn patterns of thinking that keep us stuck. You understand that, just like you wouldn't throw a five-year-old's birthday party at a five-star restaurant, you don't ask people to do transformative work in a dark hotel meeting room filled with a presentation-packed agenda.

PHYSICAL SHAPES OF COLLABORATION

By the time your partners arrive to the container of your shared work, they have accepted your invitation. They have made the journey to where you are. And they have arrived at a threshold. On the other side of that threshold could be a place where change happens, or it could be a place for more status quo. As a leader, you have the opportunity to make "in here" (read: the meeting room) a different experience, with the ultimate goal of creating positive impact "out there" (read: the world). The threshold, the physical space, and the work that happens within are the spaces of collaboration. The more conscious we are of that, the more sacred the space becomes and the more elevated the results.

There are reams of research demonstrating that our physical environment affects our moods, behaviors, and productivity. Natural light is known to boost academic performance, enhance workplace productivity, and contribute to overall psychological well-being.[42] Enclosed spaces are correlated with an increase

---

42 L. Edwards and P. Torcellini, *A Literature Review on the Effects of Natural Light on Building Occupants*, National Renewable Energy Laboratory, July 2002, https://www.nrel.gov/docs/fy02osti/30769.pdf.

in cortisol.[43] If allowed to stray outside of optimal ranges, the temperature, light, and acoustics result in increased cognitive errors.[44] "Novelty"—such as that created by unexpected activities or different visual displays—keeps us alert.[45] One study even shows the significant impact of color in a space: blue increases people's ability to use imagination and creativity to solve problems.[46] The same study shows that red increases detail-oriented activity or memory recall.

It's apparent that our brains and bodies are most effective when they are supported by their physical environment. And yet, so many collaborative gatherings are held in less than optimal spaces. Hotel meeting rooms are often the worst offenders, especially when they are windowless, lack temperature control, and are lined by carpeted (red!) walls. It's become so normal to expect this that we accept it even though we can feel how it impacts us and everyone around us.

Why don't we prioritize the physical environment? In part, many leaders don't know the impact of what seem like minor details. Or if they do recognize that it's important, they haven't fully internalized how detrimental it can be to collaborative outcomes. More often than not, they have delegated the selec-

---

43 Lars Brorson Fich, Peter Jönsson, Poul Henning Kirkegaard, Mattias Wallergård, Anna Helene Garde, and Åse Hansen, "Can Architectural Design Alter the Physiological Reaction to Psychosocial Stress? A Virtual TSST Experiment," *Physiology and Behavior* 135 (August 2014): 91–97. https://doi.org/10.1016/j.physbeh.2014.05.034.

44 Eduardo L. Kruger and Paolo H.T. Zannin, "Acoustic, Thermal, and Luminous Comfort in Classrooms," *Building and Environment* 39, no. 9 (September 2004): 1055–63. https://doi.org/10.1016/j.buildenv.2004.01.030.

45 Ramona Persaud, "Why Learning Space Matters," Edutopia, September 8, 2014, https://www.edutopia.org/blog/why-learning-space-matters-ramona-persaud.

46 Pam Belluck, "Reinvent Wheel? Blue Room. Defuse a Bomb? Red Room," *New York Times*, February 5, 2009, https://www.nytimes.com/2009/02/06/science/06color.html.

tion of space to someone else. The details seem innocuous and inconsequential.

Leaders have a critical role to play in creating an experience that draws people in from start to finish. It's easy to shy away from this role or diminish its importance. While I don't mean to suggest that leaders should spend their time scouting locations or testing the comfortability of chairs in a meeting room, they do need to cast a vision for the kind of environment that will help to accomplish their desired outcomes—and then invest in bringing that to life.

Not everyone has the resources to host a gathering like that of OC. But you don't need to rent out an all-inclusive resort for a week to create an effective collaborative space. You don't need a budget of tens of thousands or a large staff to coordinate the event either. With a little creativity and outreach, I've seen clients secure beautiful spaces by tapping into their partner networks or leveraging resources within their local community. These have included national park visitor centers, ecological centers, botanical gardens, and even presidential libraries. Each one came at no cost or were discounted because they were donated in-kind by a partner, or the venue viewed the mission of the collaboration as a worthy societal cause.

As you step into the practice of creating space, there are a few questions to consider that will help you become a masterful architect:

- **Is it the right size and shape?** Look for spaces that create intimacy without feeling overcrowded. People need to be able to see and hear one another. They need space to move about, but not so much space that they get lost in a cavernous room or are easily able to disengage by moving to the back of a large room.

- **Do we have a flexible space?** A small group focused on a shared task is different than a brainstorming session among a large group. The freedom to adjust the layout of the room is paramount to achieving the objectives of these two distinct types of interactions. Consider the nature of the work that you will be asking of participants and ensure that the room can accommodate multiple forms of engagement.

- **How will we connect with the natural world?** At a bare minimum, find a room that lets in natural light. Windows make a drastic difference in the mood and energy of participants. But beyond that, strive to select a location that includes the option of working outdoors. If our collaborations are meant to steward the future of our planet, incorporating it into our work feels necessary. It sets the tone, serving as an ever-present reminder of the importance of the work at hand.

- **Where will people sit?** This is a multilayered question. First, there is the question of comfort. Do you have seating that people can be comfortable in for an extended period of time? Second, what kind of posture do you want people to take at different points throughout the meeting? How might that impact the type of seating you provide? Finally, what value might there be in letting people self-select their seating versus a preselected strategic arrangement?

- **How do we want to make it our own?** Even the drabbest spaces can be transformed into something welcoming. A few ideas: bring in outside visuals, incorporate audio or video, stage interactive areas where people can gather between sessions, or bring color into the space through something as simple as tablecloths. Each of these suggestions can be tailored to be specific to your collaborative effort. It will go a long way to help people begin to identify with the space beyond the typical meeting room.

When I lead my clients through these questions, I often see something come alive in their eyes. As they articulate the answers to these questions, what was once "selecting a meeting room" becomes so much more. They are beginning to see the physical shape of what it means to collaborate.

SHAPING A POWERFUL SHARED EXPERIENCE

I was recently working with a client on the design of a leadership retreat. By the time we began working together, she was well past the point of sending the invitation. She had already defined the physical container. She even had the agenda defined from start to finish. Her agenda was a systematic march: presentation, discussion, decision point, repeat. And yet, her intended purpose was to collaborate and align on a strategic direction for the year. In our first meeting, she handed the agenda to me and asked if I could "just facilitate" what she had outlined.

Me: Wait, wait, wait. Let's back up to what you have here in the meeting purpose.

Her: But what about the agenda? Aren't we going to focus on that?

She was taken aback, eyes widened. I had to let her down easy when I explained that the agenda is not what defines the experience; the leader is. Leadership presence and how it's communicated through the space has a greater impact on collaboration than any agenda ever could.

I understood her confusion.

If you've been thoughtful in crafting an invitation and deliberate in creating an environment where people can do their best work, it's a natural and necessary next step to define what that work looks like. Eventually, that will take shape as an agenda, which is still only a road map. *You* are what ties together the content, the people, and the outcomes.

Your contributions to and understanding of the agenda enable you to help your partners engage effectively around the meeting's purpose once they are in the room. More important than a road map—and what is at the core of this leadership practice— is clarity on how you will lead a powerful shared experience.

Do you remember the questions that I asked as part of crafting the invitation?

- What new knowledge will be built?
- How will relationships be different?
- What action will be taken?

The answers continue to be useful. They will help you and your facilitator—should you have one—create the list of topics and flow of activities that make up an agenda.

In essence, your job is to deliver on the promise that you made in the invitation. You serve as a reminder to each and every person in the room why they are there and how important their contribution is. You have asked them to wrestle with questions that are challenging, with an environment that is not business as usual, and with issues where the stakes are high. At each turn, you'll need to know when to step in as the confident champion, the steadying hand, or the motivational force that keeps everyone together.

VIRTUAL SPACE

While digital technologies have long existed to help us collaborate, the COVID-19 world forced us into an environment where using virtual spaces to accomplish work was no longer optional. In March 2020, every organization scrambled to learn how to create environments where knowledge could be gained, relationships could be built, and action could be taken.

There has been a rapid adoption of technology, with everyone becoming comfortable and more adept at using video-conferencing software and online collaboration tools. People are beginning to understand that the virtual world can be effective. There have even been positive benefits to their personal lives, including no commute times, the ability to connect with their families more frequently, and time for deeper work.

The principles of creating virtual spaces are the same as creating physical spaces. And the reality is that we're not that great at designing spaces in the physical world that are highly functional. What I've witnessed so far is that we're attempting to translate the processes that we use when we're face-to-face into virtual environments. It's not a one-to-one exchange though. And trying to mimic what we do in real life is neither realistic nor sustainable.

Using virtual spaces requires us to be even more mindful of the practice of cultivating presence and creating space. Leaders have a responsibility for making sure that every interaction has a clear purpose. They need to encourage those around them to create supportive spaces at home that, in turn, foster a supportive environment online. We have to think about different channels for creating the shared experience. People simply can't be tethered to a computer screen for eight hours a day. Our minds and bodies will fatigue.

The container of the virtual world is much larger and with undefined boundaries. It will take a bit of imagination to build communities that feel connected enough to collaborate. This will require us to break the mold of when and where work happens. The flow of our lives is now, more than ever, governing the flow of our work. The leadership practice of creating space will necessarily be more multidimensional than the physical world. A podcast might replace a webinar. A series of leadership roundtables might replace a three-day meeting. A LinkedIn group or Slack channel might keep the conversations flowing and relationships building instead of relying on spontaneous interactions.

It's exciting to think how we might be able to use virtual technologies to gain even greater involvement in our collaborative efforts. But much like the agenda and logistics are best designed after applying the principles embodied in this leadership practice, the technologies should be selected to match the outcomes we want to create.

As a final note, we will always need face-to-face interactions in physical locations. Humans need other humans. There is nothing that can replace the energetic exchange that only happens when we are able to look one another in the eyes or simply pass time together. There are dynamics that can never be recreated or replaced in a digital world. Perhaps the separation of a global pandemic has helped us to see how important our connections are and give us even greater resolve to put this practice into play.

THE EXPERIENCE

A solid grasp on the outcomes of the meeting will guide your leadership actions throughout it: visibly, vocally, and energetically. In order to do that, it helps to understand how a leader can take the words of *knowledge*, *relationship*, and *action* and turn them into a collaborative, co-created experience. After all, your leadership empowers others to lead with you.

KNOWLEDGE: THE EXPERIENCE OF COLLECTIVE WISDOM

In most cases, we think of knowledge as something we have or don't have. Traditional educational models put a teacher at the front of the room disseminating information to his students. I have knowledge. You do not. I give it to you. You receive it. There is a transactional nature to it. Knowledge becomes concrete and unquestionable. It's one-way.

In a collaborative environment, there is no *one way* to know. Knowledge is relational and contextual. Collaborative leaders understand that there is knowledge and wisdom contained within every single person. If we don't break out of groupthink or our biases about one another, then we can't actually create new solutions. We get stuck in repeating worn-out thought patterns. But if that wisdom can be harvested wisely in a group context, individual contributions become a much more elaborate feast.

Knowledge becomes collective intelligence.

We have a host of modern examples that demonstrate what results from collective intelligence. One that you likely use every day is Google. The search engine functions so cleverly because it draws on millions of websites created by people across the globe. But even as early as 1857, we were crowdsourcing solutions. It took a team of people four decades to create a book that would contain every single word in the English language. Now you have the *Oxford English Dictionary*.

Collective intelligence becomes something like alchemy

when layered with the leadership practice of presence. When connected to their deeper purpose, each person is primed to contribute something unique that makes something completely new when combined together. Sharing presence and space activates creativity that we cannot access alone. We can generate knowledge that none of us have individually. We don't just gain knowledge; we gain wisdom.

I first learned this in the heart of the Brazilian Amazon. Recall the story about açaí distribution in chapter 1: we literally put pen to paper to map the resources within the community that were of value to them. Each person contributed their knowledge about where these resources were and their perspectives on why they were important. But it wasn't until we began to tell a story that explained the meaning of those resources that the as-of-yet unconsidered solution of bringing açaí to urban areas suddenly became so clear.

Leaders create space for this wisdom to emerge. In the design of a collaborative engagement, this means selecting processes that favor two-way dialogue over one-way presentations. Face-to-face, it means learning to ask powerful questions that draw out responses. In both cases, it means considering the diversity of our partners, what they have to offer, and how to engage them effectively.

RELATIONSHIP: THE EXPERIENCE OF CONNECTION

Turning knowledge into collective intelligence and then into wisdom requires a different level of vulnerability. This vulnerability arises when you feel free to express what you know and are willing to be empathetic to what others have to share. It's rooted in trust of the process and, more importantly, of others.

I often hear that the real work of collaboration happens in the social interactions over dinner or side conversations that happen in the hallways. Why do you think that is? It's because dinner, the hallway, or even a happy hour are smaller containers of connection. They draw people together in a different way. They also tend to draw people together who already know one another and have established trust. And when a newcomer is welcomed into that conversation, many magical insights can arise. Within these informal spaces, we tend to let our guard down. We are more comfortable and casual. We generally feel free to speak our mind and are able to listen more openly.

The lesson we can take from this is that it's important to create this same type of interaction within the more formal space of collaboration. In a meeting environment, one-on-one conversations and breakout groups provide space for people to express themselves freely. In ongoing partnership interactions, small and dynamic work groups accomplish the same. Providing structured but more intimate conversations allow people to gain greater understanding of one another. And outside of the work at hand, it's important to develop ways for people to know one another human to human. The recurring OC event fosters this by including spouses and children. Think of the culture and identity you want to create for your collaboration. Design the physical space and the methods of engagement to match it.

Here's the bottom line: building connection increases trust. Trust strengthens commitment to the shared vision and goals.

Within the larger group, trust takes more time to build. It requires courageous expression and listening. Individuals, particularly those that are introverted, may not want to speak up for fear they won't say or do the right thing. Individuals with strong perspectives may dominate the conversation, making it hard to hear the full range of perspectives. We'll explore group dynamics in a future chapter on the importance of dialogue. The key is to know how important it is for leaders to model the behavior that they want to see in others. Your presence and how you express yourself has incredible influence when it comes to creating space for relationships to build.

Here again, neuroscience proves instructive. We now know that our brains contain a set of *mirror neurons* that activate within us when we observe someone else's actions and body language. They are an internal empathy mechanism that allows us to understand what someone is thinking or feeling based on their facial expression, their body language, or the intonation in their voice. When mirror neurons are activated, we expand our capacity to understand other people's actions and the meaning behind them.

This even extends to physical sensations. Amputees often experience a phantom limb sensation. Although an arm or a leg is no longer there, the nerves that once controlled that region of the body still fire to the brain. This often manifests as pain. A set of studies examined if mirror neurons might play a role in providing pain relief for amputees. What they found is that sufferers could experience relief from pain in their phantom limbs merely by watching someone else massaging or flexing their hand.[47]

These results underscore how connected and *inter*connected

47 Vilayanur S. Ramachandran and David Brang, "Sensations Evoked in Patients with Amputation from Watching an Individual Whose Corresponding Intact Limb Is Being Touched,"

Archives of Neurology 66, no. 10 (October 1, 2009). https://doi.org/10.1001/archneurol.2009.206.

we are, mind and body. Our capacity for empathy and understanding is hardwired into our brain at a subconscious level. Your state of being and the actions that follow can create a domino effect within a group and accelerate cohesion. When you express vulnerability, vulnerability will be expressed back. When you show excitement, excitement will be returned. When you get curious, others' curiosity will spark. It won't necessarily be immediate. And it may even be resisted.

If you are consistent and patient with this practice, you'll create the space required for others to take risks intellectually and emotionally. These are the kinds of risks that lead to change.

ACTION: THE EXPERIENCE OF SHARED COMMITMENT

All collaborations drive toward action. Most leaders want to act immediately and see results quickly. The trouble with jumping to action too quickly is that it takes time for teams to calibrate to one another. As individuals, we might be deeply committed to the larger goal, but we are uncertain that others share that same commitment. Moreover, we still are in the process of understanding their perspective. It's not individual lack of desire that gets in the way of action. It's that—as individuals—we are often at different stages of committing, not just to the goal but to the process of collaboration.

It's not uncommon to see momentum building toward action only to feel some force pull us backward. Why are we stalling out? There are multiple reasons that all center around whether or not we have established shared commitment. We confuse the commitment of one person to a goal with the commitment of many. We interpret noble words and intentions with the ability to follow through. We generate excitement about creating sweeping change without holding one another accountable to the tactical details. And, perhaps most commonly and simply, we overcommit.

None of these forces are subversive moves meant to tank a collaborative process. But they underscore the importance of keeping relationships at the forefront of your efforts. When you lead a group toward shared commitment, recognize that people process in their own time and way. Just like there isn't *one way* to create knowledge, there isn't *one way* to foster commitment. In collaboration, we don't have to move forward simultaneously and in lockstep. Not everyone can or should commit to every aspect of the collaborative initiative.

Effective collaborative leaders make it known to every partner that they have full, permissive space to articulate what and how they want to contribute. Up until the point of action, your role is to ensure that enough time has been given to the experiences that deepen knowledge and relationship. You use the space to paint a picture of what could be achieved by working together. Then you take a step back. This is the point in collaboration when partners must choose for themselves. There are three questions you can ask to help guide them toward that choice:

- How do you want to contribute?
- What will keep you engaged?
- What commitment will you make?

Once you ask these questions, silence is your most powerful device. Allow people to wrestle with the discomfort of the silence. You're giving them an opportunity to reflect inwardly but also to bring that reflection forward in conversation with others. You're trusting that they will co-create an action plan that is rooted in purpose. While the first commitments may not lead to the boldest actions, they will be shared.

Momentum builds from there.

RETURNING HOME

The majestic oaks of Savannah didn't draw me in through a single tree. It was the unbroken panorama of the whole ecosystem. Generations of the right conditions had created space for each element's individual growth and interconnectedness. Some of these conditions were easy to see, while others lay invisibly beneath the surface. Together, supported by their environment and empowered through their interdependence, everything thrived.

If you are intentional about practicing the art of creating space, you will send people home with the same network of connection. They will leave with a sense that they are part of something greater, not in spite of but *because* of their many differences. That, in and of itself, is the second invitation that you extend: to continue the work together, certain that you have planted strong roots of support that will carry the collaboration forward.

Though you will cross back over the threshold of the physical space, the shared experience remains. It's what will keep you aligned to one another. It will help deliver the promise of the commitment to the larger goal. And it will make the next steps clearer, easier, and more solid.

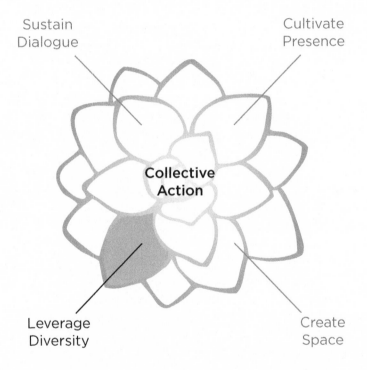

Sustain
Dialogue

Cultivate
Presence

**Collective
Action**

Leverage
Diversity

Create
Space

Chapter Five

LEVERAGE DIVERSITY

Multiculturalism is the ability to see yourself in the person most unlike you.

—SANDRA CISNEROS

A person is a person through other persons. None of us come into the world fully formed. We would not know how to think, or walk, or speak, or behave as human beings unless we learned it from other human beings. We need other human beings in order to be human. I am because other people are.

—DESMOND TUTU

Doña Irma is a small woman in her late sixties. She is of Mayan lineage, one of the few that still retains knowledge of her native language. She is a known healer. Every morning, you can see Doña Irma walking up the hills and through the streets of her town, carrying her machete and making her way toward the forest. This is Guatemala's Petén region. The sprawling jungle is steeped in Mayan legacy. The mysterious and towering Mayan temples of Tikal hint at the civilization that existed here as far back as the sixth century BC. But it's within this woman that you will find the direct link to the traditional ecological knowledge of the Mayan Empire.

By the time I met Doña Irma in Guatemala, I was three months into a six-month research investigation. My left ankle was so swollen that I couldn't fit my hands around it—and that was a marked improvement after two months of antibiotics. She looked at my ankle, then at me, and back at my ankle again. Without saying a word, I knew she disapproved. She took my hand to guide me down a path in the forest. When she finally spoke, she asked, "Tell me what happened."

Just a few weeks earlier, I had been enjoying an afternoon swim along the Esmeraldas coast in Ecuador. As a strong swimmer who loves the ocean, I found delight and adventure in long swims out to sea. This, however, did not impress my research partner. When I finally paused to look around, I saw him waving to me from the shore. Though I couldn't make out his words, I knew he was calling me in.

I swam hurriedly back to the beach. I lifted my head every so often to sight the path ahead, urged on by his frantic yet still inaudible communication. By the time I was finally close enough to hear, I was waist deep in the water. I stopped swimming and pulled my legs underneath me to stand up. The words "What's wrong?" never had the chance to cross my lips. A sharp, paralyzing pain nailed my ankle and sent shock waves up my spine. Adrenaline flooded my body, enough that I was able to take two steps forward. Then I passed out.

It was the bright lights of the hospital clinic that finally brought me back to consciousness. Miles from civilization, my partner had managed to find a doctor tucked into the Ecuadorian rainforest. She was pulling barbs out of my numbed ankle. I had stepped on a venomous stingray, and its spine was now lodged into my Achilles tendon. I felt confident in her hands. Ecuadorian-born, American-educated, and fluent in English. She sent me on my way with a clean bill of health, an arsenal of Western medicine, and the stingray's spine as a souvenir.

As the weeks progressed, the slow healing process concerned me, but I wasn't overly worried. I justified the lack of progress with the hours that I spent hiking every day in wet, rainy-season conditions. I was taking antibiotics, changing the bandages regularly, and making sure that—at the very least—nothing was getting worse.

At this point in my story, Doña Irma paused our walk. She turned to look at me again. This time, I saw disapproval *and* amusement lighting up her eyes.

As she continued to lead me through the forest, it became apparent that she was not seeing the same trees and plants that I saw—she was looking at a well-stocked pharmacy. For generations, the women in her family used the forest to cure and heal. She knew that the value of the forest extends beyond its timber value because the health of her community depends on its existence. Her job now is to make sure that information survives beyond her lifetime. And on that day, she shared it with me.

Walking from plant to plant, Doña Irma explained, "This one cures worms, this one is good to wash over a wound, and"—with a teasing smile—"this one is sure to bring love."

She harvested a few plants, intending to create a salve for my ankle. We walked back to the town in silence, and the forest seemed more alive to me than it had when we first set out. When my inflammation settled within a week's time, I thought to myself, "Damn. I should have asked for the one that brings love too."

Just as my experience swimming in the sea gave me a different perspective than my partner, Doña Irma taught me to see the forest in a new way as well. And not just the forest but human interaction with someone who, from first appearances, seemed so different than me.

My faith in Western medicine as a first line of defense was only aligned with my experience. The person in the hospital was familiar—she was "like" me in that she spoke English and held an American degree. Yet here was this wealth of generational knowledge resting in the bark and leaves surrounding Doña Irma's home, only passed along to those who would share presence and space directly with her.

This isn't a story about the best type of medicine or the safest, most reasonable perspective because collaboration is not rooted in competition or hierarchy. The purpose of collaboration is to bring all experiences together to transcend to something different—something that is inclusive and representative of the whole. Without leveraging diversity throughout that experience, we lose the beauty of our differences. We miss the perspectives that add meaning to our world, and our collaborations lose the rigor and richness that they would otherwise have.

We need each other's perspectives to help us see the unseen.

OUR BEAUTIFULLY DIVERSE WORLD

An estimated 8.7 million species make up the interconnected web that sustains us all. From plants and animals to microorganisms to the diversity of genes within each, the world we know today would not exist without their unique contributions. They weave together a global tapestry of vast and varied ecosystems.

Diversity reigns supreme on planet Earth.

The Sahara Desert and the Great Barrier Reef could not be more separate in distance or characteristics, yet we know that all ecosystems depend on one another for the flow of air, water, and nutrients between them. Science reveals that any notion we have of separateness is merely an illusion. Whether examining symbiotic relationships between species or the effects of global consumption patterns on carbon emissions, it's abundantly clear that we live in a world of interdependence.

Humans are not exempt from this interdependence. We are part of the biodiversity that has shaped the past, present, and future of our planet. We rely on functioning ecological systems as much as any other species. But beyond that, we rely on one another. We cannot celebrate the diversity of our natural world, acknowledge its inextricable connection, and simultaneously turn away from the experiential wealth that exists within our own human community.

There are more than seven billion people in our human community, and we all have something unique to offer. Each leadership practice to this point is meant to facilitate, support, and include those contributions. We cultivate presence to allow for inner stillness and recognize our distinct contribution, we use that inner stillness to create space for many voices to be engaged, and with that foundation in place, we are ready to leverage diversity. Leveraging diversity is a prerequisite to the evolution of solutions that will meet the challenges we face today. It's a practice that asks us to stretch beyond the boundaries of our own understanding, sometimes uncomfortably. It also calls us to value one another with the same reverence we hold for ecological diversity.

Our current social discourse around diversity, inclusion, and privilege is extremely sensitive. It carries an emotional charge. For that reason, the easiest solution is to avoid or disengage. We don't know how to talk about diversity. We don't share an understanding on what it is. We don't want to be judged. We don't want to be seen as misinformed. We don't know how to say, "I don't know," or "Please teach me." We don't know what our responsibility is. With all of these uncertainties, it makes this collaborative leadership practice one of the hardest to understand. It requires new learning and unlearning things we may not even be conscious of.

I tell the story of Doña Irma to illustrate the value that diversity creates for us when we are open to it. *Truly* open. One of the most common things I hear when I work on collaborative initiatives is, "We don't have all the right voices at the table. We need more diversity." That statement is necessary and applaudable, but it stops short. *Who* is representative of that diversity is never defined. *When* diversity is considered often comes only after it's glaringly apparent that it's missing. *How* that diversity is brought in is often not implemented strategically.

My hope is that anyone can see themselves in my or Doña Irma's shoes. There are so many inequities in the world, but there is also so much that we share. We are all facing the same environmental challenges and dependence on a healthy natural world. This story is an example of how diversity can become the solution, not a problem to be solved.

DEFINING DIVERSITY

At the end of the day, our ability to conserve and sustain the planet's resources boils down to the question of how we—individually and collectively—value the natural world. Those values fall along a spectrum. On one end is the belief that nature has an intrinsic worth and should be protected for its own sake. On the other end is a belief that nature has an instrumental worth that should be tied with economic, political, or social objectives. Between those two ends are a wide range of perspectives.

Your perspective and, therefore, your orientation to the environment is formed by your individual *lived experience*. The experiences, choices, and options that have shaped your life now guide how you make meaning of the world. Lived experiences encompass age, culture, ethnicity, gender identification, social class, faith or spirituality, political affiliation, power structures, and many more influences that aren't as easily identifiable. They help us to develop our view of ourselves, one another, and the world at large.

Although there are many ways to define diversity, I have found the most powerful collaborations emerge when people with vastly different lived experiences come together to create change. Defining diversity as a lived experience allows us to tap into the wisdom of the whole human being, instead of simply checking off the boxes of varied demographics. As a collaboration strategist and facilitator who has worked in many different cultural contexts, this definition allows me to remain curious about the importance of what each person brings. It helps me to surface the nuanced way we each relate to nature and to one another. Together, we are able to construct a more complete picture of our environmental challenges.

Incorporating many lived experiences into our collaborative work is a critical step to develop solutions to our global environmental challenges. Our traditional approach to conservation often discounts experience, relying solely on science-based, "expert" decision-making. While science is an incredibly powerful and necessary tool, it's limited when it neglects the rich repertoire of ways that cultures and worldviews describe, think about, and relate to nature. But it's precisely these perspectives that influence the decisions we make about the environment.

Shel Silverstein's *The Giving Tree* illustrates how perspective drives decision-making. It's the story of the relationship between a boy and a tree over the course of a lifetime. At each phase of his growth, the boy understands the value that nature provides in different ways. As a child, the tree provides him with a place to play. As a young man, she gives him apples to sell. Later, she offers her branches to him so that he can build a home for his family. And finally, when she is nothing more than a stump, she gives the old man he has become a place to rest. Though the book focuses on his individual story, it provides a metaphor for the entire spectrum of values that we collectively hold. It represents the inherent tension between our intrinsic and instrumental inclinations toward nature.

This tension will continue to challenge our collaborative efforts if we don't understand and include multiple perspectives. We will dive headlong toward solutions without untangling the extent to which "nature" means different things to different people and cultures.

A 2019 study involving researchers from thirty countries across the globe indicates the impact our differences have when framing unified environmental and conservation policies.[48] The study examined how "nature" is conceived of in more than sixty languages. Key insights underscore what *The Giving Tree* pointed to long ago, that there is a multifaceted way that we relate to nature that includes us, keeps us separate, and—in some cases—links us within an unseen spiritual dimension.

The lead researcher of this study, Dr. Luca Coscieme, reflects:

> When we refer to "nature" and "the environment," we tend to assume that every one of us has a pretty similar understanding. However, "nature" can mean very different things to a biologist studying invasive species, an art critic exposing Monet's lifework, a farmer developing his crop plan, or a kid excited to go camping with his dad.

The words we use to express our understanding of the world have

---

48   Luca Coscieme, Håkon da Silva Hyldmo, Álvaro Fernández-Llamazares, Ignacio Palomo, Tuyeni H. Mwampamba, Odirilwe Selomane, Nadia Sitas, et al., "Multiple Conceptualizations of Nature Are Key to Inclusivity and Legitimacy in Global Environmental Governance," *Environmental Science & Policy* 104 (February 2020): 36–42. https://doi.org/10.1016/j.envsci.2019.10.018.

a contextual meaning, which is shaped by our past and present experiences, our moral values, and our culture, and the same is true for the stories we tell by these words. Ultimately, the multitude of languages we find around the world results from the various ways of interacting with reality and, thus, the true meaning of the words needs to be decoded when we relate to different cultures.

We might want to recall these kinds of relations when designing environmental policies. We might also want to keep passing on values from generation to generation through stories, while listening to other cultures. Only through learning from our collective knowledge of the world will we find the major solutions to global environmental challenges we so badly seek.[49]

In other words, we cannot find solutions without a more holistic view of the problems we face. Leveraging diversity is the bridge between the previous two leadership practices and the next. It propels us toward the level of dialogue needed for effective collective action. When we weave together our lived experiences, we begin to tell our stories—even our scientific ones—in a more complete and impactful way.

UNITY IN TODAY'S WORLD

Our society is shifting as rapidly as our environment. Perhaps nowhere is that more apparent than the 2020 global coronavirus pandemic. We are keenly aware of how empty the world feels when we are in physical isolation and how rapidly nature can remind us of our connectedness. Public lands in the United States saw record-breaking numbers of visitors during the first

---

49 "Global Study Unearths Myriad Meanings for 'Nature in Different Cultures,'" Trinity College Dublin, accessed December 19, 2019, https://www.tcd.ie/news_events/articles/ global-study-unearths-myriad-meanings-for-nature-in-different-cultures/.

months of quarantine.[50] People who traditionally didn't "go outside" were suddenly desperate for places that felt open and free. It was a return to our simplest, most core need to feel part of something. Free from all other distraction, we met that need in nature.

Although that lesson surfaced in an extremely disruptive way, it also created a shared lived experience that unites us. Though the nuances of those experiences may be very different, they left us with a global yearning for shared understanding of how to resolve the chaos of our world.

Our environmental issues are just as acute, disruptive, and time critical as the pandemic, similarly uniting us within a single lived experience. Collaborations that invite diverse participation from the beginning help to define what that shared lived experience looks like. The outcome of societal and environmental shifts remains to be seen. What is clear is that the way forward—whether in a global pandemic or in conservation—is to prioritize more inclusive approaches. Diversity is essential if we want to realize the full value of what it means to work together.

No matter how far apart we are on any given issue, our values need not be in opposition. The goal is not to be the same, but to understand our differences and break down the barriers that separate us because of them. The leadership practice we explore in this chapter reveals the power of leveraging multiple lived experiences to create change. It's through this practice that we discover solutions that will advance our shared vision of a sustainable future.

---

50 "Record Visitation at Public Lands during COVID-19 Pandemic," *Smoky Mountain News*, April 7, 2020, https://www.smokymountainnews.com/archives/item/28822-record-visitation-at-public-lands-during-covid-19-pandemic.

Looking backward, it's easy to tell a coherent story of how the shifting social, political, and economic landscape of any given point in history influenced human understanding of the natural world. I told one of those stories at the start of this book. It was largely an American story that included the prevailing narrative of key turning points in conservation, land ethics, environmentalism, and sustainability.

How I tell that story and even how I write this book is influenced by my own lived experience. I am a cisgender, white woman who grew up in an upper-middle-class American family. I had resources to access an advanced education with ease. Footsteps from my backdoor lay the wildness of both a national park and a national forest.

I grew up thirty minutes from the US-Mexico border, and my formative years were greatly influenced by the Latinx culture. By the time I was in my midtwenties, I had traveled to nearly every continent on the globe to work on conservation issues at the intersection of society and the environment. Throughout my career I have more often than not been one of the few women in the room. I am only now just crossing over the age threshold where a new generation has joined the conversation. Although there are struggles that I have faced along my path, I am nothing short of privileged.

The insight of Dr. Dorceta E. Taylor sheds light on how America's conservation story changes when viewed from the vantage point of a different lived experience.

Taylor, a highly educated Black woman, is a leading expert in the field of institutional diversity and workforce dynamics in the environmental sector. She is the director of the University of Michigan's Diversity, Equity, and Inclusion Strategic Plan as well as the Doris Duke Conservation Scholars Program and Environmental Fellows Program. In her book *Power, Privilege, and Environmental Protection: Social Inequality and the Rise of the American Conservation Movement,* Taylor casts the role of Theodore Roosevelt and John Muir's work together much differently than I did. She helps us to understand the influence that race, gender, and class had during that time by pulling back the curtain on romanticized ideas of conservation agendas.

Of that, she says, "In the post–Civil War era, it became increasingly common for men to demonstrate their masculinity, wealth, and upper-class status by undertaking conquest-oriented outdoor activities such as hunting big game in the West."[51] Taylor argues that these quasimilitary expeditions justified the slaughter of Native American populations, the domination of resources like bison, and reinforced domestic roles for women.

Her book is rich with research and analysis that take us to a deeper level of understanding that the prevailing environmental narrative is not inclusive of the many experiences that shaped it. Throughout history, specific people and cultures have defined the *who, what,* and *where* of conservation work. One dominant lived experience has written that story, and it lives on in our approach to environmental issues today.

Taylor's argument doesn't negate the importance of past or current contributions. Instead, it demands and holds us accountable for the need to carve a path forward that includes

---

51 Dorceta E. Taylor, *Power, Privilege, and Environmental Protection: Social Inequality and the Rise of the American Conservation Movement* (Durham, NC: Duke University Press, 2016), 67.

dynamic sociocultural leadership in natural resource decisions. It reminds us of the cascading unintended impacts that these decisions have on underrepresented people and the ecosystems to which they belong.

This begs the questions: What story will be told a generation or two from now? Whose voice will tell it?

My hope is that the story will surpass our current perception on the role of diversity in collaborations. It will be a story in which the traditionally underrepresented voices of genders, cultures, and contexts are elevated. Instead of individual heroes, the story will center on the significant results created by collective effort. It will be a story that recognizes that the decisions we make about the use, management, and conservation of natural resources impact populations in different ways. It would concede that the costs and benefits of resource use are not equally distributed. It would prioritize environmental inequities and injustices that often go unnoticed.

The path to this future depends on diverse leadership creating the conservation agenda. But there is a critical blind spot that stands in our way: diversity is substantially underrepresented in key decision-making bodies in the environmental sector.[52] To change this will require us to upend familiar approaches to conservation, from how we foster the careers of the next generation of environmental professionals to the way we engage the public in participatory processes. A consistent focus on leveraging diversity will put us well on our way to wide accep-

_____

52 Despite constituting nearly 40 percent of the US population, minorities comprise just 12 percent of staff of both US government environmental agencies and nongovernmental environmental organizations. Taylor, DE, (2014). The state of diversity in environmental organizations (Univ of Michigan, Ann Arbor, MI).

tance of environmental policies and the achievement of key sustainable development goals. To understand the significance of diversity as a collaborative leadership practice, it's important to see the dynamics already in play that affect not only our very real future but the reality of the present as well.

THE VIEW FROM 2020

I write this book during a critical year for environmental decision-making. Under the Convention on Biological Diversity (CBD),[53] the international community will set a post-2020 conservation agenda and negotiate a framework for achieving its three main aims: the conservation of biodiversity, the sustainable use of its components, and the fair and equitable sharing of benefits arising from the use of genetic resources. The goals that are set in 2020 will impact global decisions for at least a decade to come. Although the targets set in 2011 have not yet been achieved, the post-2020 Biodiversity Framework is calling for bolder, more ambitious actions.

This is the environmental policy landscape of a new decade. But *for whom* are these decisions being made? *Who* will be responsible for implementation? *Who* will inherit the successes or failures? And *who* needs to be engaged in order to achieve meaningful, lasting results?

A few statistics to guide your thinking:

---

53 The Convention on Biological Diversity (CBD) is the international legal instrument for "the conservation of biological diversity, the sustainable use of its components and the fair and equitable sharing of the benefits arising out of the utilization of genetic resources" that has been ratified by 196 nations. It's first iteration was created in 1992 at a global summit in Rio de Janeiro, a landmark effort to align international interests around shared environmental issues.

- The United States will be "minority white" by 2045,[54] and the population identifying with two or more races is the fastest-growing racial/ethnic group between 2010 and 2020.[55]
- 75 percent of the global workforce will be made up of millennials by 2025.[56]
- 97 percent of the world population growth will be in developing countries by 2035.[57]
- Although global gender parity is not expected to be reached for over one hundred years, women steadily continue to gain representation in senior political, private, and public sector leadership positions.[58]

More broadly speaking, our overall population is on the rise. By 2030, it's expected to reach 8.6 billion, and by 2050, 9.8 billion.[59] By 2030, there are expected to be forty-three cities with more than ten million inhabitants, and by 2050, 68 percent of the

---

54 William H. Frey, "The US will Become 'Minority White in 2045, Census Projects," Brookings Institution, March 14, 2018, https://www.brookings.edu/blog/the-avenue/2018/03/14/the-us-will-become-minority-white-in-2045-census-projects/.

55 Leslie Aun, "What the 2020 U.S. Census Will Tell Us About a Changing America," PRB, June 12, 2019, https://www.prb.org/what-the-2020-u-s-census-will-tell-us-about-a-changing-america/.

56 Peter Economy, "The (Millennial) Workplace of the Future Is Almost Here—These 3 Things Are About to Change Big Time," *Inc.*, January 15, 2019, https://www.inc.com/peter-economy/the-millennial-workplace-of-future-is-almost-here-these-3-things-are-about-to-change-big-time.html.

57 "97% of Population Growth to Be in Developing World," Consultancy.uk, June 24, 2015, https://www.consultancy.uk/news/2191/97-percent-of-population-growth-to-be-in-developing-world.

58 *Global Gender Gap Report 2020*, World Economic Forum, 2019, http://www3.weforum.org/docs/WEF_GGGR_2020.pdf.

59 "World Population Projected to Reach 9.8 Billion in 2050, and 11.2 Billion in 2100," United Nations, June 21, 2017, https://www.un.org/development/desa/en/news/population/world-population-prospects-2017.html.

human population will live in urban areas.[60] This increase in population and urbanization will continue to shape the multitude of lived experiences and, in turn, the way each of us values, understands, and uses our natural resources.

Society is more diverse than ever before and changing rapidly. Voices that were once marginalized are gaining strength. New lived experiences are coming into existence before our very eyes. Structures that once favored previously dominant lived experiences are breaking down. Even within each demographic category, the research shows a wide variance of perspectives, making it that much more difficult to assume understanding and that much more imperative to seek out broad and active engagement.

What's more is that the research is clear: diverse, inclusive teams and organizations deliver better outcomes.

- **There is a direct correlation between diversity and innovation.** Immigrants to the United States obtain 28 percent of high-quality patents (defined as those granted by all three major patent offices), though they constitute only 18 percent of the twenty-five-and-older workforce. They are also more likely to become Nobel Laureates in physics, chemistry, and physiology or medicine.[61]
- **Gender and racially diverse management teams perform better.** Gender diverse executive leadership teams financially

---

60 "68% of the World Population Projected to Live in Urban Areas by 2050, Says UN," United Nations, May 16, 2018, https://www.un.org/development/desa/en/news/population/2018-revision-of-world-urbanization-prospects.html.

61 Jay Shambaugh, Ryan Nunn, and Becca Portman, "Eleven Facts about Innovation and Patients," Brookings, December 13, 2017, https://www.brookings.edu/research/eleven-facts-about-innovation-and-patents/.

outperform their competitors by 21 percent while ethnically/culturally diverse teams outperform by 33 percent.[62]

- **Diversity attracts talent.** Remember that by 2025, millennials will make up 75 percent of the global workforce. Millennials view diversity as more than race, demographics, equality, and representation. They see it through the lens of varying experiences, different backgrounds, and individual perspectives. Forty-seven percent of millennials consider diversity when conducting a job search, and 74 percent consider their organization more innovative when it has a culture of inclusion.[63]

- **Inclusive teams make better, faster decisions.** Teams that follow an inclusive process make decisions two times faster with half the meetings. Their decisions meet or exceed desired outcomes 87 percent of the time.[64]

- **Inclusive teams are more resilient in the face of uncertainty and disruption.** Following the 2009 financial crisis, publicly traded companies with inclusive cultures saw a 14.4 percent gain in stock performance compared with the 35.5 drop in performance by the S&P 500. The research focused on whether groups like women, people of color, LGBTQ people, and people with disabilities consistently reported positive experiences and whether those typically underrep-

62 Vivian Hunt, Lareina Yee, Sara Prince, and Sundiatu Dixon-Fyle, "Delivering through Diversity," McKinsey & Company, January 18, 2018, https://www.mckinsey.com/business-functions/organization/our-insights/delivering-through-diversity#.

63 "The Deloitte Global Millennial Survey 2020," Deloitte, https://www2.deloitte.com/global/en/pages/about-deloitte/articles/millennialsurvey.html.

64 Eric Larson, "New Research: Diversity + Inclusion = Better Decision Making," *Forbes*, September 21, 2017, https://www.forbes.com/sites/eriklarson/2017/09/21/new-research-diversity-inclusion-better-decision-making-at-work/#5bdb32a24cbf.

resented or disadvantaged groups were well represented at various levels of the company.[65]

Although it doesn't take much imagination to understand why diversity strengthens results, the quantifiable indicators of its importance are overwhelming and mounting. The longer we think of diversity as an initiative, campaign, or program, the more we delay leveraging its critical contribution. Whether societal or ecological, diversity fortifies every pathway to a sustainable future for all.

The participatory process for developing the post-2020 Biodiversity Framework acknowledges the importance of a "whole society" approach. Specific attention is being paid to the engagement of diverse perspectives from indigenous and local communities; integrating women and gender issues; facilitating participation from different levels of government, civil society, and the private sector; as well as connecting with youth. But when the ink has dried and new targets are set for 2050, the true test will be whether we move beyond merely paying attention to the need for diversity or embodying it as an active leadership practice. If we do, we will break through stuck paradigms and patterns that have held us back for far too long.

STRUCTURAL DYNAMICS

Robert Stanton was the first African American Director of the United States National Park Service, appointed by President Clinton in 1997. Before then, his thirty-five-year career had spanned from Grand Teton National Park in Wyoming

---

65   Ed Frauenheim and Nancy Cesena, "New Study Reveals That Diversity and Inclusion May Be the Key to Beating the Next Recession," *Fortune*, December 20, 2019, https://fortune.com/2019/12/20/diversity-inclusion-key-to-beating-next-recession/.

to the Virgin Islands National Park in the Caribbean to the National Capital Region in Washington, DC. Among other accomplishments, he was known for his expansion of public–private partnerships and recognition of the contributions made by minority populations to American cultural heritage. While his accomplishments stand on their own, they have even greater significance when understood within a historical context.

Stanton was born in 1940 in Fort Worth, Texas. He grew up in Mosier Valley, a community settled by freed slaves in the late 1800s. He attended a segregated elementary school. His mother was a short-order cook, and his father baled hay for local farmers. By the time Stanton was eight, he was driving a tractor for his father in the hay and cotton fields of Texas. Although he describes his childhood as one spent outdoors, there was just one local park that he—or any other Black person—was allowed to visit.

He didn't come from a family of means, but by excelling in school, he received a scholarship to attend Huston-Tillotson College in Austin. A historically black college and university (HBCU), Huston-Tillotson was one of several academic institutions targeted by the National Park Service to recruit minority candidates for seasonal employment. Stanton had never visited a national park. Prior to the Civil Rights Act of 1964, many people of color were legally barred from, or segregated at, public recreational sites, including national and state parks.[66] But Stanton was struck by the majestic vision of the western parks that the recruiter painted that day in 1962. He was selected for a summer seasonal position at Grand Teton

66 Susan Shumaker, "Untold Stories from America's National Parks: Segregation in the National Parks," PBS, accessed September 22, 2020, http://www.pbs.org/nationalparks/media/pdfs/tnp-abi-untold-stories-pt-01-segregation.pdf.

National Park in Wyoming. Over one thousand miles away from home, Stanton would become part of the first integrated National Park Service workforce.

Of the approximately fifty African American students recruited to the National Park Service from HBCUs that summer, only half showed up for duty.[67] Even with the promise of employment, significant barriers stood in the way of these students accepting their positions. They had no frame of reference and no one to advise them on how to navigate the logistical and financial burdens of a temporary move, what they might expect life to be like in a completely different cultural and geographic region, or what it meant to work as an employee of a national park—particularly as part of an integrated work situation.

In an oral history interview, Stanton reflects:

> My situation, I think, perhaps mirrors some of the circumstances that confronted some of these other students. First, you had to provide for your own transportation, in my case from Texas to Wyoming. So that meant trains and bus fare. Also, you had to have your uniform purchased before you arrived on duty. And then you had to have sufficient resources to carry you through for at least a week, possibly two weeks before you got your first paycheck. And the only people who could possibly assist me with those expenses were my mother and relatives, and nobody had $250 to loan me or give a student to go out West.[68]

Stanton was able to address financial barriers with the help of

---

67 Kathy Mengak, *Reshaping Our National Parks and Their Guardians: The Legacy of George B. Hartzog Jr.* (Albuquerque: University of New Mexico Press, 2012).

68 Janet A. McDonnell, "Oral History Interview with Robert G. Stanton," National Park Service, 2006, https://www.nps.gov/parkhistory/online_books/director/stanton.pdf.

a prominent white farmer and dairyman for whom he and his father had worked. The man cosigned a loan for $250 at a local bank, and Stanton paid it back in two installments. But it took courage and fortitude to overcome the obstacles of being one of only a few Black people, not only in the National Park Service but in Wyoming. While government officials might have seen his employment offer as an opportunity, what they didn't realize is that they were asking him to navigate—geographically, socially, politically, economically, and emotionally—rigid structures that would stand in his way throughout his career. And he was doing it alone.

One of the primary drivers that influenced Stanton's decision to pursue his career in the National Park Service was his experience with the Grand Teton staff. He reflects:

> It was not so much the grandeur, the natural and magnificent beauty of Teton, year-round snowcapped mountains, etc. But what was really defined for me was the quality of the professional staff at Grand Teton. One has to realize that the Park Service, and particularly the parks where African Americans were assigned, they had little to say about this. The [Secretary of the Interior] said in effect, 'You are going to have African Americans working as rangers in the parks.' So, in some parks, unfortunately, because I met some of the rangers who worked that first year, too, they were merely accommodated by the professional staff. But I can say without any hesitation that the three African Americans, including myself, working at Grand Teton in '62 were warmly and truly welcomed to the workforce. It spoke volumes about the quality and the professional integrity of those who were there at Grand Teton in 1962.[69]

---

69 Ibid.

These are the humble beginnings of a distinguished career. Nine national parks and seventeen natural heritage areas were established during Stanton's tenure as Director of the National Park Service. He played a key role in the passage of the National Underground Railroad Network to Freedom Act of 1998, which funded preservation of sites and education efforts. He challenged Park Service leadership to work outside of the organization and park boundaries with local communities, other governmental agencies, and the private sector, recognizing the importance of engaging in dialogue with partners to achieve conservation objectives.

Stanton carved out his own legacy, but his entry point into a life of civil service came as the result of a crack in a once impenetrable wall. In 1961, newly appointed President Kennedy established the quiet but powerful Subcabinet Group on Civil Rights. With public opinion running against the civil rights movement, Kennedy charged the group with using executive authority to initiate policy changes that did not require Congressional approval. The government launched its first affirmative action program in April of that year, forging an agenda to counter racial discrimination and to employ minorities in federal agencies. It was at this time that Secretary of the Interior Morris Udall began recruiting students from HBCUs like the one Stanton attended and began desegregating all national parks.

Though we have come a long way since the 1960s, we have not come far enough.

The irrefutable evidence of police brutality against minorities, at first, may seem unrelated to environmental issues, but the heartbreaking flood of stories we see today reveals the powerful influence of the same social, economic, and political structures that Stanton faced. We live in a world where public policies, institutional practices, cultural representations, and other norms reinforce inequity—sometimes intentionally and sometimes unintentionally. We cannot deny that certain types of people or groups are disproportionally restricted in their opportunities.

Creating opportunities is important, but it doesn't ensure that we all are taking continued responsibility to ensure those opportunities can be accessed. Instead, it creates a false sense of security that we are tackling injustice. The opportunity itself creates an "us-them" dynamic and an excuse to walk away, believing that "we" have done our part. All of us are responsible for breaking down these preventative structures and rebuilding a more equitable world.

Dismantling the structural dynamics that limit diversity in collaboration does not happen with a single policy, program, person, or step. Affirmative action opened the door for Stanton into the National Park Service, but there were other factors at play that encouraged him to invest in a lifelong career:

- The president signed an executive order that, though limited in its scope of authority, initiated a federal affirmative action plan.
- The efforts of a recruiter inspired a vision of the western parks so magical that Stanton would say yes to a seasonal position.
- The community—both at home and in Wyoming—provided the resources and emotional support that enabled his success.
- The continued integration of the federal workforce shaped a growing cultural consciousness, eventually leading to the passage of the Civil Rights Act of 1964.

These were the individual seeds of change, but no *one* thing created the structural change that facilitated Stanton's journey. Additionally, his unique place in history does not guarantee that the door remains open for diverse leaders to walk through in the future.

We can meet the basic requirements for representation of diverse lived experiences within our collaborative initiatives. We can expand beyond those basic requirements to consider how we invite people to participate and the processes we use to engage them throughout our work together. But we also must address visible and invisible constraints—ranging from lack of time, access, and resources to sociocultural frames—that favor a predominately white and/or upper-middle-class experience.

Much of the future of our natural world rests in the hands of people and communities who have not yet had their voices heard. Their silence has been a detriment to our future. Our collective potential will only be realized when we all recognize our shared responsibility.

DIVERSE, NOT DIVIDED

The experience of being human is singular and shared, and though there are variations on those experiences, we are all reliant on one another and the resources of this planet for survival. Each of us understands and values relationships differently, our individual lived experiences shape our perspective and actions, and our social, economic, and political structures uniquely affect our ability to influence outcomes. Despite all of the complications these differences can create, there is some startlingly good news as well: the richness of our diversity creates powerful points of synergy.

A 2019 study of the views held by those working to protect the natural world found that there was substantial agreement on the goals of conservation: (1) maintaining ecosystems, (2) securing public support, and (3) reducing the environmental impact of the world's richest.[70] The study posits that, perhaps, we are not as far apart as we think we are and that our differences are not irreconcilable. Perhaps there isn't a single choice to be made as to the value of nature. We agree upon the common aims of conservation. Where we diverge is in how to achieve those aims. We are missing an explicit accounting of our values.

From intrinsic to instrumental and everywhere in between the two ends of the spectrum, our views are as diverse as we are. That diversity is an asset. It can only heighten our understanding of the multitude of ways we can work toward conservation goals.

All four collaborative leadership practices teach us how to recognize our interdependence and interconnectedness. But it's in the mastery of leveraging diversity that we break through the walls that keep us separate.

UNDERSTANDING AND BREAKING BIAS

Collaborative leaders that pay attention to the leadership practices of presence and space are primed for creating more inclusive conversations. These practices allow for openness, safety, and trust that can empower all voices. But they quickly unravel without acknowledgment of one simple truth: we all have biases.

---

70 Chris Sandbrook, Janet A. Fisher, George Holmes, Rogelio Luque-Lora, and Aidan Keane, "The Global Conservation Movement Is Diverse but Not Divided," *Nature Sustainability* 2, no. 4 (April 9, 2019): 316–23. https://doi.org/10.1038/s41893-019-0267-5.

Bias can lead to outright discrimination, acrimonious debate, or complete disenfranchisement. Or it may show up more subtly, like the incorrect pronunciation of a name to whom we give the floor to speak. We can emphasize the importance of diversity through our words, but it's our actions that reflect mastery of diversity as a leadership practice.

More importantly, we cannot eliminate our biases through training. Training can help us see the system that needs to be dismantled. But we need to take the next step of addressing policies, practices, strategies, and norms that limit our ability to deliver results. In every collaborative initiative I have participated in, we think about this same kind of dismantling but applied to the environmental issue at hand. Why, then, do we not immediately evaluate these same concepts in our human-to-human interactions?

Biases are *unconscious* drivers that influence how we see the world. Cognitive scientists have identified 150 possible biases. Biases are an adaptation. They free up precious mental energy so that we don't have to make every decision fresh. To have a bias is not a moral judgment. It's part of being human. There is no part of our day that isn't influenced by our biases. From something as simple as turning on a computer to selecting a movie to the way we start a conversation, our biases take charge.

It takes a heightened self-awareness (and a decent amount of humility) to recognize our own biases. I recently came across a political satire cartoon that depicted a couple sitting on the couch watching a political debate. The man said to his wife, "Funny how it's only the people that I disagree with who are biased." Isn't that the truth? It's easier to recognize bias in other people than within ourselves. No one *wants* to be biased—at least, not overtly—but we are, nonetheless. Each and every one of us has unconscious biases that impact all of our decisions.

Many of our unconscious biases work in our favor. Our brains synthesize and store previous knowledge to help us move rapidly through the world. You only need to burn your hand once on a hot stove to learn to steer clear of all sources of heat in the future. In other words, you don't need to stick your hand in a fire to learn that it will also burn you. Your brain has already created a shortcut to help you avoid pain. This is an example of an unconscious bias that allows you to make quick, effective decisions without taxing your mental resources.

The challenge is that, while the neural circuitry of our brain works hard to make our lives easier, it can't distinguish between situations where biases are helpful or unhelpful. In the case of collaboration, we can counter these biases by including a broad range of options, strategies, and approaches. Leveraging diversity is a powerful way to consider complex environmental issues in fresh ways from multiple angles. But if our brains take shortcuts, as they naturally will, we shut down the possibilities that different lived experiences generate. Additionally, because many of our biases are unconscious, we are not even aware that we are acting upon them.

Collaborations are strengthened when they address biases at the outset so that they don't go unnoticed or unaddressed as we strive to do the same for the barriers that stand in the way of achieving conservation goals. We leverage diversity when the whole becomes more than the sum of its parts. But we cannot create something whole when we aren't learning how our biases drive our actions.

We cannot ignore the existence or importance of diversity. We cannot afford to be ignorant about our biases. Yet, when it comes to collaborating on environmental issues, there is evidence that we are doing both.

Daniel Kahneman, renowned psychologist and winner of the Nobel Prize in Economics, explains the two systems that drive the way we think in his book *Thinking, Fast and Slow*:[71]

1. **System One is fast, instinctive, and emotional.** It's the memory of the hand on the hot stove when faced with a fire. Kahneman explains that this system of thinking is more influential than you think, guiding almost all of your regular judgments and choices.
2. **System Two is slower and deliberate.** It involves thinking that is more complex, requires concentration, and involves thought processing. Although it tends not to be as creative as the first system, it leads to more rational and logical thinking. The focus required to increase your natural walking pace is an example of how you tap into this second system.

---

71 Daniel Kahneman, *Thinking, Fast and Slow* (New York: Farrar, Straus and Giroux, 2013).

SYSTEM 1	SYSTEM 2
FAST	SLOW
Zzz UNCONSCIOUS	CONSCIOUS
AUTOMATIC	EFFORTFUL
EVERYDAY DECISIONS	COMPLEX DECISIONS
❌ ERROR PRONE	✅ RELIABLE

Daniel Kahneman, *Thinking, Fast and Slow*, (New York City: Farrar, Straus and Giroux, 2013)

We like to think of ourselves as conscious, deliberate human beings that spend most of our time operating from System Two. Unfortunately, this is not the case. Take the financial crisis of 2008. Kahneman illuminates that unhelpful biases driven by System One led the world to ignore evidence that the practices in place were going to have devastating long-term effects. Did the warmth and charm of Bernie Madoff lead us to believe that everything would turn out okay? Of this kind of thinking, Kahneman says that we have "almost unlimited ability to ignore our ignorance."[72]

While we recognize the value of working together, developing partnerships, and building coalitions, we are "thinking fast" when we pull these collaborations together. We haven't slowed down our thinking enough to see the magnitude of underrepresentation within them or to consider the effort needed to broaden representation.

---

72 Ibid., 201.

A 2014 study of the state of diversity in environmental organizations provides insight.[73] As part of this study, 191 conservation and preservation organizations were asked about their collaboration, coalition, and network-building activities over the last three years:

- 72 percent of the organizations reported collaborating with other organizations frequently or very frequently.
- 40 percent reported that they did not collaborate with any low-income group, and 20 percent seldom collaborated with such groups.
- 36 percent did not collaborate with any ethnic minority groups, and 24 percent seldom collaborated with such groups.
- Less than 3 percent of organizations collaborated with low-income groups very frequently.
- Less than 4 percent of organizations collaborated with ethnic minority groups very frequently.

Diversity is a value that we espouse as essential to collaboration, but are we actually putting it into practice? This study demonstrates that we are failing in race and class alone, and those are just two of many lived experiences that are essential to successful collaboration. Are we aware enough of our biases to do something about them?

To be human is to have biases. No one is exempt. We cannot eliminate them. We can only accept that they are always operating in our first system of thinking. While this awareness may help leaders realize that they might be biased in one way or

73 Dorceta E. Taylor, *The State of Diversity in Environmental Organizations* (Ann Arbor, MI: University of Michigan, School of Natural Resources & Environment, July 2014), http://orgs.law.harvard.edu/els/files/2014/02/FullReport_Green2.0_FINALReducedSize.pdf.

another, it does little to offer them a way to identify, interrupt, and redirect their thought process. This is why bias training is not enough to make real change.

What an individual cannot do for himself, a group *can* do. Collaborative leaders can draw on one another to identify biases and develop strategies to address them. They can build a culture that acknowledges the importance of working through biases. To do this, the most effective approaches focus on changing processes, not changing minds.

THE SEEDS MODEL

In an after-hours conversation with one of my clients, I was struck by my own bias. This client is a white, senior-level executive at a major conservation organization. My experience with him is one of an extremely passionate and caring human being who is driven by his deep love of our natural world. He is highly educated and has used that education to make a real impact throughout his career. I have known him for nearly a decade, but I had never heard the story of his upbringing. What I learned that night was that his success was hard won. He grew up in a rural, poor area of the South. Neither of his parents were college educated. Both worked long hours to make ends meet. Despite all of this, he also recognizes that as a white male, there were structural dynamics in place that did facilitate his success.

As he told me about his childhood experience, so much clicked into place for me about the choices that he has made throughout his life. Because we share so much in common both in and out of a professional setting, I assumed that our lived experiences were more closely aligned than they are. That assumption not only prevented me from knowing and appreciating him on a deeper personal level, but it made me realize that I had missed an opportunity to leverage his lived experience in our work together. He brings perspective that is often missing when teams of highly successful people decide to collaborate. It's a needed perspective, too, as the economic gap between the rich and the poor only widens.

We should all have more conversations like these with our colleagues. To affect the environmental change that is needed, we have to understand and break the biases that keep us at odds about the "right" path to take. In my work, I help my clients to have the kind of authentic, open dialogue that leads to System Two thinking. Through the design and facilitation of that dialogue process I use a model developed by David Rock of the Neuroscience Leadership Institute that helps groups reduce unconscious bias.

The SEEDS Model categorizes 150 biases into five broad categories:[74]

- **Similarity: We prefer what is like us over what is different.** Humans are highly motivated to see themselves and those who are similar in a favorable light. Similarity biases instinctively create "ingroups" and "outgroups." We tend to see those in the outgroup or on the margins more skeptically.
  - The way to address similarity biases is to actively seek out common ground with people who appear different.
- **Expedience: We prefer to act quickly rather than take our time.** Our brains are primed to be right. We have a built-in need for certainty. In that need for rightness and certainty,

74 Heidi Grant Halvorson and David Rock, "Beyond Bias: Neuroscience Research Shows How New Organizational Practices Can Shift Ingrained Thinking," Strategy+Business, July 13, 2015, https://www.strategy-business.com/article/00345?gko=ed7d4.

we can rush to judgment or action without considering all of the information available to us.

- The way to address expedience bias is to slow down and gather more information.

- **Experience: We take our perception to be the objective truth.** Our experience shapes our brain circuitry to understand the world as a direct and objective representation of reality. These biases are similar to visual illusions (i.e., two lines are the same length even though they look to be different lengths). Even if you know that you are looking at an illusion, it's difficult to change your perception of it.
    - The way to address experience bias is to work with others to gain outside perspective and develop group strategies to challenge our thinking.
- **Distance: We prefer what's closer over what's farther away.** We prioritize what is nearby. This includes physical space, time, and even ownership. We assign greater value to those things that we perceive to be close to us, simply because they are close.
    - The way to address distance bias is to develop strategies to identify, review, and prioritize those things that are farther away from us.
- **Safety: We protect against loss more than we seek out gain.** Humans are highly sensitive to expectations of loss. Negative information tends to motivate action more than positive information. This is an evolutionary adaptation that helped us avoid predators. Safety biases slow down decision-making and hold back healthy forms of risk-taking.
    - The way to address safety bias is through visualizing the positive outcomes of risk.

This model is a powerful tool for collaborative groups that are committed to leveraging diversity. Understanding that these biases are always running in the background enables groups to challenge them with intention. I encourage my clients to adopt group norms that hold everyone accountable for spotting biases as they arrive. In doing so, they have a safe and shared approach to create a culture of inclusivity.

At the heart of the SEEDS Model is a three-step process for creating that approach:[75]

1. **Accept** that people and systems are deeply biased and do not know it.
2. **Label** the biases likely to occur in any given system or decision, based on the five major categories into which they fall.
3. **Mitigate** bias by attacking it with strategies that go directly to the core mechanisms underpinning that bias.

Taking the time at the outset of a collaboration to adopt this model as a cultural practice and intentional process within every conversation is critical to leverage diversity. David Rock emphasizes through his research that no one can mitigate bias alone. It takes an entire group using common language around bias to build stronger relationships, make better decisions, and outsmart groupthink.

THE NECESSITY OF OUR DIFFERENCES

Some of the most surprising lessons that I have learned about the connection between diversity and environmental issues have come from my time living and working in the American South. There is a land ethic here that has been shaped by centuries of

---

75 "Make Informed, Effective, and Confident Decisions when It Matters Most," NeuroLeadership Institute, accessed September 22, 2020, https://neuroleadership.com/scalable-learning-solutions/decide/.

cultivating, managing, and conserving the region's rich natural resources. There is also a history of racial tension. Both of these things have shaped how people relate to nature and one another. Southern culture is, in part, defined by a sense of place. The land is the connective tissue that helps to unite a diverse population that is still wrestling with the wounds of slavery and decades of explicit and structural racism.

Yet it's our differences and divides—not our similarities or common history—that build strong collaborations.

Diversity forces us to pause, to look for points of connection, and to work together on a shared vision. When that vision is conservation, I've seen my southern clients bridge conservative and liberal politics in ways that have been impossible for nearly every other topic we face. They've been able to bring together organizations that primarily value the environment as instrumental to economic gain and organizations more focused on the intrinsic leanings of traditional conservation agendas. While they don't always see eye to eye, they are able to recognize that they cannot avoid one another if they ever want to achieve their ultimate goal.

The environment is the issue that speaks to every lived experience.

There is much that we have yet to wrestle with to understand, appreciate, and act upon our intersections. But we are seeing more evidence that we can gain ground even when it seems we hold irreconcilable differences. Amid the global pandemic, racial divides, and election-year rhetoric of 2020, the United States Senate passed one of the most significant pieces of conservation legislation in recent decades. It was a bipartisan bill called the Great American Outdoors Act, which called for funding the Land and Water Conservation Fund at $900 million and provided billions to address maintenance backlog issues for public lands. At the time of this writing, that bill has passed through the House of Representatives and is headed toward President Trump's desk. However, as the bill was being created, there was already work afoot to ensure its enactment. Senator Cory Gardner, a Colorado Republican, knew that to gain Trump's support required him to share in the vision around which Democrats and Republicans had already aligned.

Gardner told Trump that signing the bill would be a conservation accomplishment on par with that of Theodore Roosevelt in the early 1900s. He showed him pictures of the lands he would be protecting. Upon seeing these, the president said of the bill, "That is beautiful. Put [the bill] on my desk and I will sign it."[76] Trump shifted his perspective and intent to deny the bill and joined in support of it.

Leveraging diversity, breaking down structural dynamics, labeling, accepting, and mitigating our biases—it all means that sometimes we find ourselves face-to-face with people and politics we don't (and don't want to) agree with, like, or trust. But we need one another. And just as importantly, we need to *understand* one another. We build that understanding, word by word, through the fourth and final collaborative leadership practice: sustain dialogue.

---

76 Carl Hulse, "Senate Moves Toward Preserving Public Lands, and Political Careers," *New York Times*, updated June 11, 2020, https://www.nytimes.com/2020/06/08/us/politics/senate-public-lands.html?smtyp=cur&smid=tw-nytpolitics.

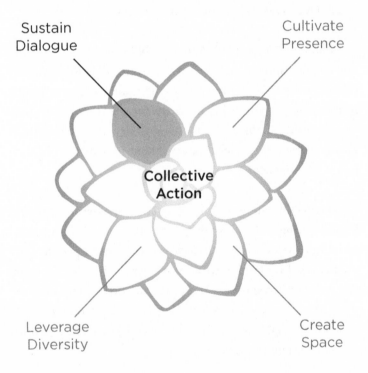

Sustain
Dialogue

Cultivate
Presence

Collective
Action

Leverage
Diversity

Create
Space

Chapter Six

SUSTAIN DIALOGUE

If you talk to a man in a language he understands, that goes to his head. If you talk to a man in his language, that goes to his heart.
—NELSON MANDELA, SOUTH AFRICAN ANTI-
APARTHEID REVOLUTIONARY

The year is 1939. The Nazi Party is taking hold in Germany. World War II is just beginning. In California, a theoretical physicist, David Bohm, is on the rise as a leading researcher in the fields of quantum mechanics and relativity theory. He has been recruited by Robert Oppenheimer to join his group at UC Berkeley. Later, Oppenheimer will ask Bohm to join his team on the Manhattan Project. Bohm will be denied because of his affiliations with the Communist Party. Despite this, Oppenheimer will use Bohm's research in the creation of the atomic bomb.

According to colleagues, including Albert Einstein, Bohm was renowned for his sensible interpretation of quantum mechanics. But his work would later turn to deeper dimensions of consciousness and spirituality. He was a friend of Krishnamurti, one of the first modern Indian sages to bring the idea of enlightenment to the Western world. This influence coupled with his scientific grounding would lead him toward interests in neuropsychology. A paper called "On Dialogue" became one of his most prominent works. In it, his definition of dialogue gives light to the difference between the kind of conversations we often engage in versus what is needed to create something new, interesting, and meaningful:

> I give a meaning to the world 'dialogue' that is somewhat different from what is commonly used. The derivations of words often help to suggest a deeper meaning. 'Dialogue' comes from the Greek word *dialogos*. Logos means 'the word' or in our case we would think of the 'meaning of the word.' And dia means 'through'— it doesn't mean two. A dialogue can be among any number of people, not just two. Even one person can have a sense of dialogue within himself, if the spirit of dialogue is present. The picture or image that this derivation suggests is a stream of meaning flowing

among and through us and between us. This will make possible a flow of meaning in the whole group, out of which will emerge some new understanding. It's something new, which may not have been the starting point at all. It's something creative. And this shared meaning is the 'glue' or 'cement' that holds people and societies together.

Contrast this with the word 'discussion', which has the same root as 'percussion' and 'concussion.' It really means to break things up. It emphasizes the idea of analysis, where there may be many points of view. Discussion is almost like a ping-pong game, where people are battling the ideas back and forth and the objective of the game is to win or to get points for yourself. Possibly you will take up somebody else's ideas to back up your own—you may agree with some and disagree with others, but the basic point is to win the game. That's very frequently the case with discussion.

In a dialogue, however, nobody is trying to win. Everybody wins if anybody wins. There is a different sort of spirit to it. In a dialogue, there is no attempt to gain points, or to make your particular view prevail. Rather, whenever any mistake is discovered on the part of anybody, everybody gains. It's a situation called win-win, in which we are not playing a game against each other but with each other. In a dialogue, everybody wins.[77]

I came to Bohm's philosophy about midway through my career. Yet it's undeniable that my work is a legacy of his thinking. "On Dialogue" presents many of the themes we have already discussed: the importance of creating space for connection (specifically, in a circle), the way our nonverbal cues influence our connection, the idea that creative and collective thought

---

77   David Bohm, *On Dialogue*, 2nd ed. (New York: Routledge Classics, 2004).

originates when people act from a state of flow, and the way that our biases and assumptions influence our actions. He reminds us that dialogue is a process that takes time, practice, and the consideration that everything is an experiment. There are no guarantees about what will happen as a result of that process.

I'll never know for sure, but piecing together the timeline of his life, I have to believe that his contributions to the atomic bomb caused an existential reflection about whether there was a better way to achieve peace. He was firm in his convictions that there was no *one* truth, despite his scientific training. He even predicted that someday science and art will merge:

> This division of art and science is temporary. It didn't exist in the past, and there's no reason why it should go on in the future. The ability to perceive or think differently is more important than the knowledge gained.[78]

We need leaders who are willing to perceive and think differently. The amount of time and resources that we've spent investing in technologies is enormous. And the results are staggering, evidenced by the fact that the phone I carry every day is more powerful than the first spaceship. Yet we are communicating and solving problems in the same way we did centuries ago.

We're facing our own series of atomic bombs today. Nearly every structure and old way of thinking no longer works. If dialogue is the key to unlocking the doors to the future, it's time we learn how to do it.

---

78 John Horgan, "David Bohm, Quantum Mechanics and Enlightenment," *Cross Check* (blog), *Scientific American*, July 23, 2018, https://blogs.scientificamerican.com/cross-check/david-bohm-quantum-mechanics-and-enlightenment/.

Our final collaborative leadership practice is to *sustain dialogue*. It embodies all three of the previous practices. It cannot exist without them. It builds upon them and reinforces them. If you are cultivating presence, you're priming yourself for dialogue. When you shape your space and craft your invitations, it's to facilitate dialogue. And dialogue is richest when it's among a diverse range of perspectives.

The practice of dialogue requires that we come back to the other three practices over and over again. When we sustain its practice throughout the life of our collaborations, we move collective action forward.

A teacher of mine has a saying: "There is no safe way to be great. And there is no great way to be safe. Transformation requires courage. There is no way around it." When we step into this final leadership practice, the only thing that matters is courage. Courage to speak up. Courage to speak with our most authentic voice. And courage to tell the truth.

If we are practicing *presence*, *space*, and *diversity*, that courage will come easier, but it will never come easy. We often think of collaboration as an exercise in getting along, agreeing, and reaching consensus. I hope by now it's clear that collaboration is something different. It's an act of being in relationship with one another in a way that exposes ourselves. We take that risk so that we can begin to see all the angles and intersections of our greatest challenges. When we speak with courage and allow others to do the same, we transform ourselves, others, and the world around us.

Robert Kegan, the same researcher who gave us the theories of adult development presented in chapter 2, and his research partner Lisa Lahey argue that just being able to see the system makes us less captive to it. This is key to collaboration. First, we see the human system of our collaboration. What is important to each individual? What is their purpose or vision? What are their doubts or fears? Second, through that understanding of our cocollaborators, we see how the system defines the issue at hand. What factors are at play socially, economically, ecologically, politically, spiritually, etc., that influence our outcomes? Being able to see these systems allows us also to see the potential and the limitations in them, freeing us to make new choices.

Dialogue provides that freedom. It's the practice that can help us achieve great visions and unimagined futures. But to get to the heart of dialogue requires that we take the risk of saying what we really think and feel. It's the practice that most outwardly demonstrates how well we have learned and integrated the previous lessons of collaborative leadership. We know we have achieved the mastery of dialogue when there is nothing that is nonnegotiable or untouchable. Then, and only then, we demonstrate how courageous we're willing to be in the pursuit of our collective vision.

DEFINING DIALOGUE

It's been fifty years since Bohm published "On Dialogue," and dialogue is still not our primary mode of communication. Even in arenas where transformational change is needed, including in our personal lives, we lack dialogue. Instead, we have conversations, discussions, debates, and negotiations.

We often start by asking the question, "What needs to happen?"

This is a question that automatically narrows our thinking. Dialogue asks, "What do we need to understand before we take action?" It gives us a greater field of vision, opening up awareness that there is something beyond what we can immediately see.

UNDERSTANDING THE DIFFERENCES BETWEEN DEBATE, DISCUSSION, AND DIALOGUE

DEBATE	DISCUSSION	DIALOGUE
Succeed or win	Present ideas	Broaden our own perspective
Look for weakness	Seek answers and solutions	Create shared meaning
Defend our opinion	Enlist others	Express paradox and ambiguity
Focus on "right" and "wrong"	Share information	Bring out areas of ambivalence
Search for flaws in logic	Give answers	Discover collective meaning
Deny other's feelings	Avoid or discount feelings	Explore thoughts and feelings

Source: Adapted from Ratnesh Nagda, Patricia Gurin, Jaclyn Rodriquez, and Kelly Maxwell, "Comparing Debate, Discussion and Dialogue," University of Michigan, 2008, https://depts. washington.edu/fammed/wp-content/uploads/2018/06/3d-HANDOUT.pdf.

The goal of dialogue is not action. It's a process designed to create shared meaning. Shared meaning doesn't negate your experience or mine. Dialogue fosters a give-and-take between the individual and the collective, an infinite loop that expands the longer we sustain it. Attaining consensus can only lead us to a single answer, a finite point. We've spent decades now trying to find *the one* answer to address our environmental challenges. Dialogue teaches us that there are many ways forward and that they are not in competition.

If we were to distill dialogue down into a formula it might look like this:

dialogue = the quality of listening + the quality of advocacy and inquiry

Dialogue is the very heart of collaboration. Our primary reason for coming together is not just to solve a problem but to learn from each other and to create new outcomes. To create better dialogue, we have to improve the quality of each of its components: listening, courageously revealing our experience and perspective, and asking good questions.

THE QUALITY OF LISTENING

Think of a time when you expressed something of importance to you, and the person that was listening truly understood. More than just the words you were saying, this person grasped some greater sense of how you felt and who you were. You were able to speak *to* (not at) this person. You likely left this conversation feeling supported, seen, and perhaps even with a sense of relief. Instead of fighting to be heard, your words flowed with ease.

Pause to reflect. What made that conversation different? What was the person doing or saying that let you know they understood?

It's a rare gift to have someone listen to you this deeply. Listening isn't a skill that is taught to us or incorporated into leadership courses. We are accustomed to communicating at a level that hovers at the surface or transmits information. We also don't ask to be heard in this way or take the risk of initiating conversations like these. Usually, we reserve this type of communication for our most trusted circles.

Pause to reflect again. What happened after the conversation you just recalled? Think about how you felt, how your relationship to that person changed, what mindset shifts occurred on either of your parts or what new ideas or actions emerged. There is almost always something new that emerges out of quality listening.

Listening requires that we momentarily suspend our inner voice to be present to another person, give them space for expression and bring forth the whole of their lived experience. Too often, we listen with the goal of responding. We make it about us. From a place of excitement, we might want to share how we have had a similar experience. From a critical mind, we might want to sway someone to see things differently. From a place of validation, we might want to cast a vote with our agreement.

Quality listening prioritizes the person who is speaking, with curiosity and all five senses engaged. You notice the impact that the person is having on you without jumping in to react. Your senses provide the clues to what is being expressed beyond words.

When you pay attention to all of the nuances and layers that come through another's communication, it's hard to be distracted by our own thoughts, beliefs, and assumptions.

Listening doesn't only happen in one-to-one interactions either. Improving collaboration requires us to learn how to listen more globally. While one person may be speaking in any given moment, listen for how that interaction impacts the energy of the group. You'll begin to notice the subtle shifts that are happening between and around you, things like whether tension or anticipation is building. If you listen closely enough, you can sense what wants or needs to happen next. You'll have an instinct of whose voice will best move the dialogue forward.

I liken listening to the experience of watching a movie with compelling characters, sweeping visuals, and a stellar soundtrack. We can pay attention to the person talking and the storyline. Or we can step back to see the surrounding artistry that is moving the people and plot forward. Our experience of what is immediately in front of us becomes richer and stronger when we listen in different ways. Our appreciation for the whole of the movie and what it took to create it expands. We understand that there have been many contributions, all coming from individuals in collaboration with one another, to bring that story to life. If we are moved, the story lingers with us long after the time we invested in watching it. In a way, we become co-creator, telling the story to others and encouraging them to share in the experience. We become a full participant, not just a viewer.

The last dynamic of listening comes from within because speaking is an act of courage. There is a time to return to self, tuning into your inner voice and acknowledging that your thoughts, ideas, feelings, assumptions, beliefs, and opinions matter too. Without them, you become a passive observer, and you'll never know the impact of your contribution.

THE QUALITY OF ADVOCACY AND INQUIRY

There is a way to bring your voice into the room authentically yet respectfully. To do this requires an understanding of the difference between advocacy and inquiry.

Advocacy is the act of promoting our view. Inquiry is the act of asking questions to search for information. When used effectively, advocacy and inquiry allow for the diverse lived experiences within a collaboration. They create space for learning to occur. And they cultivate presence within the group that emboldens our vision.

Quality listening predicates quality advocacy and inquiry because our natural tendency is to communicate in a way that promotes our view on what needs to be accomplished and how it needs to be done. But if we are listening to our internal voice, our collaborators, and have more global awareness of the dialogue as a whole, we enter into dialogue more thoughtfully. We activate the System Two thinking that Daniel Kahneman encourages.

There are productive and unproductive ways to use advocacy and inquiry. Learning how to use them productively amplifies our impact as leaders. Instead of communicating in a way that diminishes trust and creates confusion, we learn to communicate in ways that allow everyone to expand their thinking, to be compassionate, and to act wisely.

ASSUMPTIONS IN DIALOGUE

Throughout this book, I have cautioned you to examine and question assumptions that prevent you from being in full collaboration with others. However, there are assumptions that can help shift your mindset in a way that leads to quality dialogue. Recall that our biases stem from the basic principle that the brain likes to be right. If we let this base instinct take over, we enter into conversations with the stance that others either already agree with us or, through persuasive argument, can be convinced that our views are correct.

With that in mind, there are some assumptions that are helpful in dialogue:

- Assume others see things that you cannot see.
- Assume you see things that others miss.
- Assume others are expressing themselves in ways that make sense to them.
- Assume that everyone is capable of using a full range of leadership styles.
- Assume that you have a role to play in lessening stress responses in others.

PRODUCTIVE AND UNPRODUCTIVE ADVOCACY

Advocating productively requires awareness of yourself and others, skills in speaking and listening, sensitivity, respectfulness, and humility. Advocacy moves the collective thinking of a group forward. It also helps reveal and resolve potential flaws in reasoning, gaps in information, and conflicts in goals.

The key to productive advocacy is to help others understand the rationale behind your thinking. People want to understand how you have arrived at your conclusions, whether through data or concrete examples of personal experience. Instead of presenting your ideas as *the truth*, encourage others to challenge your views through inquiry. Reveal any doubts you might have or any inferences that you may be making. Acknowledge to yourself and others that you are limited in your perspective.

Unproductive advocacy prioritizes being right or looking good over everything else. Typically, when people advocate in this way, they only state their conclusions and not the steps in their reasoning. Ideas are presented as final products. This discourages different perspectives, ideas, and asking questions that refine our thinking.

PRODUCTIVE AND UNPRODUCTIVE INQUIRY

Productive inquiry originates from quality listening. Through listening, we learn what questions to ask and how to ask them. Yet it's not the questions themselves that are important. The questions are simply the tool that we use to engage everyone in learning. Inquiry allows the group to see new and varied perspectives. It also builds trust and alignment between the group.

Genuine curiosity is the foundation that productive inquiry is built upon. The skill that is most important to productive inquiry is learning to ask open-ended questions. Good questions are catalytic and expand the potential responses. They allow you to test your understanding of what other people are saying. They probe at how others arrived at their views. They offer others the opportunity to challenge your view. And they solicit input from everyone.

Unproductive inquiry uses questions to manipulate communication. Examples of this include asking leading or rhetorical questions, asking questions to prove others wrong rather than to learn, couching statements as questions, or using questions to show others' lack of knowledge.

LOW-QUALITY INQUIRY	HIGH-QUALITY INQUIRY
Do you understand what I am saying?	What is your reaction to what I am saying?
Don't you agree? Don't you think it would be better if...?	In what ways is your view different? My view is X. How do you see it?
Did you do that because of X or Y?	What was your thinking on that? What led you to do what you did?
Why can't you do X?	What would it take to do X?
Why didn't you just tell me?	What led you to not tell me? Did I contribute to your not speaking up, and if so, how?

Source: David Coghlan and Mary Brydon-Miller, eds., The Sage Encyclopedia of Action Research (Washington, DC: Sage Reference, 2014).

BALANCING ADVOCACY AND INQUIRY

In every dialogue, there is a need to balance advocacy and inquiry. When advocacy is more present than inquiry in dialogue, it prevents groups from understanding their differences. High degrees of advocacy tend to discount the range of perspectives, which can lead to conflict or withdrawal. When inquiry is high without advocacy, it's difficult to know where anyone stands.

Being able to recognize when advocacy and inquiry are unbalanced helps us to course-correct. The most effective collaborative efforts operate with high advocacy and high inquiry. But we can sense when that isn't happening. It's easy to spot where the imbalance is when we look at the results that it produces:

- High advocacy and high inquiry lead to collaborating and learning.
- High advocacy and low inquiry lead to forcing and pushing.
- Low advocacy and high inquiry lead to easing and accommodating.
- Low advocacy and low inquiry lead to withdrawing and withholding.

Our leadership style often dictates our preference to use advocacy or inquiry within a collaboration. There are many frameworks that assess leadership style, many of which you are likely aware of or have been exposed to. Since it's rare that I walk into the room with the advantage of having everyone's Myers-Briggs assessment results in front of me, I use a simpler leadership model to guide my clients to create balanced advocacy and inquiry.

The model is David-Kantor's Four Player Model, which describes four leadership archetypes and their role in promoting advocacy and inquiry within a group.[79] As you read through the descriptions of each, you'll likely be able to identify which is dominant for you and the elements of others that you embody (or not). You can also use this model to consider what archetypes exist within your current collaborative efforts, which ones are missing that could provide that balance, and how to navigate any type of group interaction.

THE FOUR PLAYER MODEL

The four leadership archetypes can be thought of as a diamond that follows the cardinal directions. For each archetype, there is the characteristic description, the primary function that it serves in the dialogue, and its primary intention. Even though we have natural tendencies toward a certain leadership style, the power of advocacy and inquiry is that they serve as a tool to help us move between the other three styles, depending on what's needed within a whole group interaction.

Kantor suggests than in any social system or group, there are

---

79 David Kantor, *Reading the Room: Group Dynamics for Coaches and Leaders* (San Francisco: Jossey-Bass, 2012).

four core acts that create the balance of advocacy and inquiry. I describe them archetypally because it's not just the act itself but the leadership qualities that enable action to happen. See if you can spot where you lean.

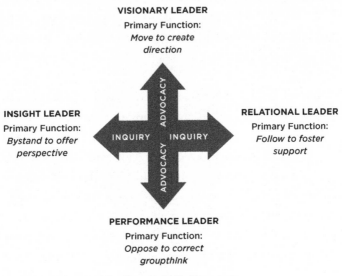

Adapted from David Kantor's Four Player Model, The Kantor Institute

THE VISIONARY LEADER

This is the motivating force within a group. Sensing what is needed, their leadership presence helps to create synergy and shared purpose among the group. They are articulate, inspiring, and charismatic. They can often be heard saying, "I have an idea!" In a place of stress, they might become fearful or worry that their ideas aren't good enough or won't be accepted by the group. Moments of stress might sound like, "I can't do this anymore."

The primary function that the Visionary Leader plays within a group is to create *movement*. Without visionaries, there is no *direction.* This is their primary intention, whether in a moment of healthy or stressful expression.

THE RELATIONAL LEADER

This is the leader who prioritizes relationships. They are the peacekeepers and are empathetic and kind. They pay attention to the feelings, emotions, and energy of individuals and the group. They want all perspectives to be heard. You might hear them say, "I like your idea." Their gift is one of appreciation, holding everyone in esteem. On their shadow side, they may be overwhelmed by controversy or discord. Their desire to value relationships may get in the way of necessary tension. The stress can sound like, "Let's all calm down and get along."

The primary function of the Relational Leader is to *follow*. Without followers, *nothing gets done.* Their intent is to foster support for an initiative in order to bring it to completion.

THE PERFORMANCE LEADER

Performance leaders are highly driven toward accomplishment. This is the person who loves knowing exactly what the strategy is and how it's going to be put into action. They are excellent at setting boundaries for themselves and the group. They enjoy creating checkpoints along the way to an outcome. They're heard saying, "What's the plan?" They counterbalance the Visionary Leader by challenging the group to think critically and practically. When they engage in dialogue in an expansive way, their contributions help to define a manageable framework forward. However, they can get frustrated with too much expansion. In this case, their stress manifests as impatience or anger. It might sound like, "Can we just get to the solution?"

The primary function of the Performance Leader is to *oppose* ideas. Their intent is not to be confrontational but to elicit critical feedback. Without them, there is no *correction* to groupthink.

THE INSIGHT LEADER

They see all the possibilities. They stand back in observation. As they are doing this, they are building a mental map of how the perspectives in the room connect with one another. They often can see what others cannot. They may be perceived as quiet or shy, but make no mistake, they are quite busy taking it all in. They might be heard saying, "I can see how these things relate." When they actively participate, they bring new perspectives to light and shift the group toward innovation. Their stress is often driven by not feeling important. It may sound like, "No one is hearing me." In those instances, they may begin to manipulate the group through passive-aggressive statements or offering up an idea that is meant to create chaos.

The primary function of the Insight Leader is to *bystand*. They process from the sidelines before they offer what they are seeing. Without them, the group misses seeing a bigger picture or critical elements of a smaller one. Their intent is to provide *perspective*.

THE LEADER'S ROLE IN BALANCING GROUP DYNAMICS

Just as we need a balance of advocacy and inquiry, we need a balance of Kantor's Four Players. Without the four leadership styles present, it's impossible to have a balance of advocacy and inquiry. Visionary and Performance Leaders are the advocates. Whether they are offering ideas or challenging one, they have a stake in the direction of the collaboration. Relational and

Insight Leaders are the ones that inquire. They tune into the dynamics of the group and demonstrate how those dynamics contribute to the whole.

As collaborative leaders, we have a responsibility to learn how to embody each of these archetypes. Although you might be naturally inclined in one direction, the health of your collaborative efforts depends on your ability to move between them. That also means you become skilled at moving between productive advocacy and inquiry. By identifying what is missing—either in leadership or communication styles—you will be able to step up to give the group the energetic push it needs.

We strengthen our individual and collective growth when we are willing to adopt different—even if uncomfortable—stances to sustain quality dialogue. No leadership style should be prioritized or idealized over another. Nor should advocacy be prioritized over inquiry. We must learn to integrate and use all of these principles.

FACILITATING DIALOGUE

The components of dialogue are straightforward. It's easy to say, "Learn to listen, present your viewpoint, and ask good questions of others." But we know that dialogue is the first thing to break down when tension is high or relationships aren't yet strong. It's easier to devolve into a shadow side of leadership when the entire group isn't committed to sustaining dialogue.

In the early stages of collaboration, dialogue requires guidance. There should be someone whose vested interest is in the group itself and strengthening the ability of its participants to work together. At least one experienced facilitator is essential. Their role should be to realize the subtle differences between dialogue and other forms of group processes. As an objective participant, the facilitator leads from behind to assist the group with staying true to their commitment to listen, advocate, and inquire in productive ways. The facilitator supports the group in forming its identity and establishing a collaborative culture that includes all four leadership practices, including dialogue.

Ideally, the way to begin a collaboration is to talk about dialogue. Some level of training is needed for the group to understand what it is and why it's important. The group has to buy into dialogue. Part of this conversation includes a hard examination of what kind of collaborative effort this group wants to invest in. Important questions need to be answered:

- Where do we want to be on the spectrum of collaboration?
- Are we interested in creating transformative change?
- Are we willing to put in the time and effort as leaders to make that change happen?
- Do we recognize that it requires us—individually and collectively—to focus on our growth as leaders?

I have seen so many groups launch collaborative efforts with the goal of transformation but without understanding the leadership work it takes to get there. They have awareness that their environmental issue is challenging but don't have a sense that the solutions require a different way of leading from within and in concert with others. There are even times when clients come to me seeking facilitation support, but their mental model about what facilitation is looks more like timekeeping and monitoring the conversation.

Dialogue facilitation is much more than that. Collaboration is much more nuanced than that.

Ultimately, my job is to teach leaders how to sustain dialogue on their own. That should be the role of any facilitator or consultant. I want my clients not to need me eventually. But because dialogue is not our primary mode of communication in the world, I hold them accountable to it. The world is growing in complexity. There is no better time to learn and commit to this practice.

QUALITIES OF A DIALOGUE FACILITATOR

The following qualities were identified by an international team of dialogue practitioners with years of experience using dialogue to create social change:[80]

- **Strong listening skills.** Facilitators need to be able to listen closely during all phases of the process. This enables the facilitator to design an appropriate process, to mirror to participants what is going on, and to help the group become more aware. Strong listening skills depend partly on the ability of facilitators to let go of their own agendas.
- **Personal awareness and authenticity.** As much as paying attention to what is going on in the group, dialogue facilitators need to be able to understand what is going on within themselves when in the group. This is quite a profound metaskill of facilitation, which is particularly important in less structured, more open-ended processes and more psychologically oriented processes. Facilitators are essentially holding the group and need to avoid projecting their own issues and insecurities onto the group

---

80 Marianne Mille Bojer, Heiko Roehl, Marianne Knuth, and Colleen Magner, *Mapping Dialogue: Essential Tools for Social Change* (Chagrin Falls, Ohio: Taos Institute Publications, 2008): 24–25. https://www.taosinstitute.net/product/mapping-dialogue-essential-tools-for-change-by-marianne-mille-bojer-heiko-roehl-marianne-knuth-and-colleen-magner.

while they also deal with projections of the group toward them. Personal awareness relates to the ability to be honest about one's own limitations (what one is and isn't capable of) and the willingness to hand over a process to participants when they are ready.

- **Asking good questions.** Asking good questions is a form of art. Effective questions will wake participants up, link into what they care deeply about, and make visible their interdependence in finding the answers. They will surface new insights participants hadn't thought of before to understand the issue in focus. A simple phrasing of a question determines whether people feel hopeless and despairing or curious, energized, strong, and excited.

- **A holistic approach.** Being able to assess which method to use in a given situation, or whether one's preferred method is applicable, requires a facilitator to understand the particular context. Taking a holistic approach is all about being able to see patterns, helping the group make connections as they work, and recognizing that multiple intelligences are at work. The more the whole person can be invited into a dialogue, the more equitably people will be able to engage.

RETURNING TO PRESENCE

There is no linear path to collaborative leadership. Whether we've had a successful experience with dialogue or we're struggling in the midst of one, there will always be a call to return to presence. Space will always be the container of our interactions. Diversity will inform them. These practices are intertwined and continually feed into each other from all angles.

As you step into dialogue, always check in with your sense of presence first. Return to your intentions: What are you curious about, and what do you need to know to see things differently?

What flaws are there in your thinking, and what is the collective thinking of the group?

In a group that is becoming more conscious in its leadership and collaborative in its approach, breakthroughs happen with greater frequency and ease. We understand that relationships are the key component of our work. Dialogue is the practice that pushes us over the line to take collective action. We're evolving into a new story that we're shaping together.

Chapter Seven

TAKING COLLECTIVE ACTION

None of us—singly or sitting in committee—can possibly blueprint a specific 'plan' for resolving the environmental crisis. To pretend otherwise is only to evade the real meaning of the environmental crisis: that the world is being carried to the brink of ecological disaster not by a singular fault, which some clever scheme can correct, but by the phalanx of powerful economic, political, and social forces that constitute the march of history. Anyone who proposes to cure the environmental crisis undertakes thereby to change the course of history. But this is a competence reserved to history itself, for sweeping social change can be designed only in the workshop of rational, informed, collective social action. That we must act is now clear. The question which we face is how.

—BARRY COMMONER, CELLULAR BIOLOGIST,
PROFESSOR, AND POLITICIAN

Stories don't have a middle or end anymore—they usually have a beginning that never stops beginning.

—STEVEN SPIELBERG, DIRECTOR,
PRODUCER, AND SCREENWRITER

As a species, we understand change through stories. We learn through myths, through adventures, and through our own personal cautionary tales. Everything that humanity has learned about who and what we are has come through story. It's why we resonate with the campfire—our stories came long before the scientific culture that we know today.

It's time to consider that we're telling an epic tale that never stops beginning. If we are to transform the way we collaboratively lead environmental change, we have to change our perception that our vision and goals for the future have an end point. We also have to rethink who the authors and characters really are. As we come into ever-increasing mastery of *presence*, *space*, *diversity*, and *dialogue*, we'll discover that there are no singular protagonists or villains, victims, or heroes. To take collective action means that we coauthor the story. In doing so, we commit to growth that moves us closer to our desired outcomes. But we recognize that the next generation will tell the story anew. Collaborative leadership can reshape the structure of our environmental narrative.

On the TEDx stage in 2010, Nancy Duarte famously uncovered a connection between story structure and the patterns underlying great speeches. As an expert on persuasive presentations, she described the architecture of motivational communication and how a familiar framework—beginning, middle, end—creates resonance. To illustrate just how powerful our stories can be, she analyzed the "I Have a Dream" speech and the speech Steve Jobs gave with the release of the iPhone.

The first thing she examined was the vocal frequencies of each speech. In both speeches, then in subsequent speeches that she continued to analyze, there was a similar vibration shared between them. The voices moved up and down in a cadence, and the content structure moved as well. Every word and every line pulled the listener along in a way that was not only heard but *felt.* The changes could be seen in the frequency bands mapped on an electromagnetic spectrum.

The speeches that sparked new societal outcomes followed a pattern: What is the current reality and what could it be? Back and forth, over and over, the speakers oscillated between the status quo and an inspiring future, outlining a "new bliss" that was progressively revealed during the speech. Not only were the listeners moved in those moments, but entire movements were built around them. The masses took collective action based on the structured speech of one individual.

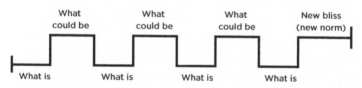

Nancy Duarte, "The Secret Structure of Great Talks," TEDx, November 2011, https://www.ted.com/talks/nancy_duarte_the_secret_structure_of_great_talks?language=en

Following in the footsteps of the growing understanding of the importance of story, I began to wonder: If a single speech can propel a movement, is there also a structure to collective action? Is there a pathway we can expect to encounter on the collaborative leadership journey? If we think about collaboration as a story, how does it change our approach? How much more comfortable can we be with experimentation and creating shared meaning when we believe—as Martin Luther King said—"the arc of the moral universe is long, but it bends towards justice"?

If Spielberg is right, that stories don't have an ending anymore, then the possibilities become even more exciting. We can pen the world's narrative, move toward our next evolution, and never close that door entirely. We can set off on a collective adventure—realizing that we will continuously be called to describe what is and what could be. The practices of collaborative leadership provide us with the preparation we need. With them, we'll have the tools to work together to meet the forces of change as long as the Earth is ours to explore.

LEARNING FROM THE HERO'S JOURNEY

Connected to Duarte's analysis of persuasive communication lies another structure that has existed throughout human history. Joseph Campbell, an American professor of literature, identified a central story that defines human experience. He coined it "the hero's journey." It's now the famous guideline for modern storytelling, largely influenced by Carl Jung's views on myths.[81] Campbell's exploration of archetypal stories of heroes throughout history, from religious theology (Buddha, Christ, Moses) to Greek Mythology (Odysseus), identify the hero being called out into the world on an adventure, facing challenges and temptations, being guided by a mentor, claiming victory, and then returning home with new wisdom and lessons to be shared.

The hero's journey always begins with a seed of purpose. There is a deeper meaning that we're drawn to fulfill. Not long after, we realize that we are uncertain how to fulfill that destiny, so we find a mentor or they find us. They help to solidify our commitment, equip us with the tools and wisdom that we'll need, and guide us across the threshold to the unknown world.

81 Joseph Campbell, *The Hero with a Thousand Faces* (Princeton: Princeton University Press, 2004).

Even though we're supported at this stage, the unknown world is filled with struggle. There are trials and tests and inevitable failures waiting, tempting us to give up. Our commitment and resilience are tested in small, mundane ways, like Mr. Miyagi's tests with Daniel in *The Karate Kid*, or in bigger ways, like Frodo's many setbacks in *The Lord of the Rings*. Every failure is another lesson and another chance to stand up and try again. If we're willing to face what seem like insurmountable failures, our commitment is renewed.

To continue on the journey, there must be a final loss of ego, a letting go of the idea of being heroic and a surrender to the present. The old version of ourselves dies—and someone new, with all of the lessons of the trials and failures we experienced, emerges. When we let go in that way, we give space for new ideas and solutions to emerge. A revelation happens that tells us who we are and what our gifts are to be used for. A new way of being and acting takes the place of the old paradigms and beliefs. While it may be our purpose that called us out on the adventure, the journey allows us to yield to our role as servant leaders acting for the greater good.

Since collective action has no formula, the hero's journey is a metaphorical way to set expectations for the experience of personal and group change. The same structure that has guided us throughout human history can teach us to be present to our reality while anticipating what will be required of us. It's why the collaborative leadership practices are so vital to success. They are navigational tools that keep us oriented along the way.

Additionally, the hero's journey offers us a way to reconceptualize the journey we are on—a call to collaboration in service of a more sustainable world. There is a tension waking us up to the reality that our normal, everyday lives are not so normal anymore. We feel a pull toward resolution now more than ever, and we have a choice. We can sit in that tension and ignore it, or we can answer the call to set off toward the horizon. Not everyone will opt in. But when enough of us do, we propel society—and the environmental issues we care about so deeply—forward.

THE COLLECTIVE HERO

At some point in your life, you have lived a form of this story. And any time we come together to collaborate, we are—largely unconsciously—attempting to write this story together. Our personal heroes' journeys are inextricably connected to how we take collective action. Individually and together, we are drawn to change the course we are on.

For those of us who have accepted the call and are leading environmental change, the challenges of this unknown world are immense and growing. The intensity of change elevates our sense of urgency. More and more, we are looking to one another to see what other leaders might have to offer. Up until now, the trails we've chosen have been separate but parallel. In seeking collective action, we've begun to look for the switchbacks that lead us to points where we intersect. We've accepted that we need help, and we're drawn to collaborate.

For years, we've looked to technical solutions instead of being adaptive. We've invented technology that has helped us advance but allowed it to replace our pursuit of relational integration. Our death and rebirth are in progress—the loss of old structures and the death of our need to be the hero. As we evolve toward collaborative leadership, we are also evolving Campbell's traditional, triumphant story structure.

With each passing year, we grow more impatient with results and refuse individual heroic, egoic attempts at change. The call for collaboration is deafening. It echoes and reverberates in our hearts and minds. And the most hopeful examples of *what could be* come when we witness communities pulling together. Imperfectly and messily, they are actualizing the change that we've been wondering how to create. The collective hero is emerging.

Popular culture reflects this too. The hero's journey is being recast to emphasize that we are stronger together than we are alone. It's societal evolution that reflects our unconscious desire for something different. Collaboration is what wins the day in the *Avengers* assembling or the *Stranger Things* kids finally meeting back up with their various pieces of the puzzle to solve the unknown force that is working against them. Even in *Star Wars*, the story that is most often used to exemplify the hero's journey in modern times, we see an evolution within the latest films. It's the telling of the complete resistance movement rather than Luke Skywalker's path alone.

All of us are hungry to see that people can come together to overcome a string of increasingly demanding challenges because that's what we're up against now in every aspect of life. Collective action requires that we let go of winners and losers, forget about beating the villain, and realize that our story never reaches the conclusion of living happily ever after—but it can move us forward to powerful possibilities.

THE STRUCTURE OF COLLECTIVE ACTION

When we turn back to nature, our ultimate teacher of evolution, we find a different metaphorical structure to represent collective action. You've been following this structure throughout this book represented visually by the spiraling leaves of a succulent.

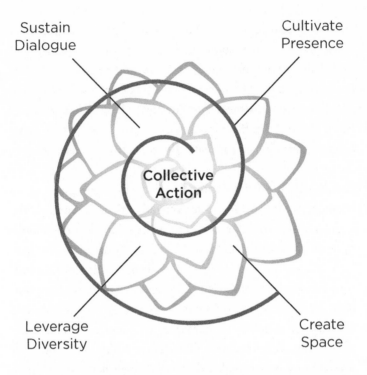

Sustain Dialogue

Cultivate Presence

Collective Action

Leverage Diversity

Create Space

I could have chosen any number of spirals that exist in nature, but this one seemed most compelling. It represents continual growth. It has adapted with precision. It thrives when it bends toward the light. It's layered and multidimensional, but the integrity of the structure reinforces itself. It stores precious resources within every cell of its being. It draws upon them when its surrounding environment lacks nourishment. It demonstrates that survival is possible in the harshest of conditions.

Spirals are sacred symbols that represent the journey of life as it unfolds. They are one of the most common patterns we see in nature. The Fibonacci sequence, or the golden ratio, is a series of numbers in which each number is the sum of the previous two (0, 1, 1, 2, 3, 5, 8…). It forms a geometry that can be found on the petals of a flower, the arrangement of leaves along a stem, in seashell formations, and even in parts of the human body, such as our five fingers.

Consciously or not, humans are programmed to understand and respond to the golden ratio. The Acropolis of Athens, the Mayan temple of Chichén Itzá, and the Buddhist stupa of Borobudur are just a few of many examples where humans have mimicked it in architectural design. Beethoven composed his Fifth Symphony using the same pattern. And Leonardo DaVinci was well known for his use of the Fibonacci sequence throughout his work, including the Mona Lisa.

I offer this as a structure, not as a definitive end, in order to invoke a more visceral understanding of our work. Each leaf contributes to the whole, just as each leadership practice makes collaborations stronger. Each layer of outgrowth represents an expansion of our impact. Instead of the closed loop that the hero's journey depicts, the spiral can lead us leaf by leaf, layer by layer, step by step toward collective action. Those steps are concrete but continuously expanding. They make the intangible tangible.

Keep this metaphor in mind as we—finally—put together all of the pieces and learn the stages of collective action: alignment, strategy design, experimentation, the pause, and emergence.

ALIGNMENT: THE DECISION TO ACT

Creating alignment within a collaboration is the first stage of our journey. There are three things which are critical to align to at the start of any collaborative initiative. First, all participants must have a shared vision for change. Second, they must have a common understanding of the problem. Third, they must have a joint approach to solving it through agreed-upon actions.

It takes time to create alignment. The leadership practices not only accelerate that timeline but also make the process richer and relationships more cohesive. Ensuring that everyone has a common understanding of the problem has been, in my experience, the most challenging part of any collaboration. It's often skipped over, with stakeholders assuming that the problem is obvious to all.

If there is a recognition that everyone may not understand the problem in the same way, what quickly surfaces are the nuanced ways that each person sees the issue and ultimate goals for success. We need presence to understand a shared purpose. We need space to build a powerful experience. We need diversity to include a 360-degree view of the issue. And we need dialogue to motivate action.

It's important to remember that each partner is already investing in solutions and activities that are part of the solution. If you are to gain their participation, it must be clear that aligning with a collaborative effort will create even greater value to their organization. They are likely to have to redirect their resources to contribute to a bigger vision. As such, every element of the collaboration is being run through an evaluation filter. They are asking themselves, "Are the differences between our view of the issues a detriment to my work? Or could collective action contribute to my individual and organizational probability of success?" The decision to act happens once partners determine that they are an integral part of the collaborative structure.

As more multisector and public-private partnerships come into existence, alignment to a shared vision, core definition of the problem, and joint actions is the difference between merely coordinating efforts and transformational collaboration. To get this stage requires precision, which can often stir up fear that a narrower scope of work will limit engagement. It won't. The precision is what helps you develop the compelling invitation.

Alignment breeds commitment, but it doesn't create certainty. This will be another hurdle you should expect to face during this stage. In the language of the hero's journey, alignment is the call to adventure, and the commitment is to the uncertain. There will be a necessary shedding of self-importance. You'll be challenged to maintain a curious mindset. Your traditional approaches will be questioned. And the strategies you develop will not look like anything you have seen before.

STRATEGY DESIGN: MAPPING THE UNKNOWN WORLD

Strategy design is a progressive process. It's the power source for collective action. Every partner brings strengths and strategies to the table that differentiate one person from another. Collaborative efforts strive to leverage each partner's unique contribution. This process is one where we transition from isolated to holistic planning efforts that are reflective of the complexity of the issue at hand.

As the health of our relationships within the collaboration strengthen, we keep our eyes focused on systems-level change. It's important to remember that the system is not fixed. External societal, political, and environmental conditions will evolve, as will our understanding of collaborative leadership. The strategies that we choose, emerge from an evaluation of these changing conditions and the interplay of our individual activities. Through this exploration, we will see gaps in connectivity as well as existing techniques that are working but could be amplified. The design of strategies should feel amplifying, not limiting.

That being said, there should be no fewer than three and no more than five shared strategies. The more strategies we have, the more we dilute our capacity for collective action. We slip away from our commitment to the collective journey, reverting back to multiple heroes' journeys running in parallel. This puts us in competition for resources, limits our impact, and weakens our ability to utilize the full range of expertise available to us.

Funders of collaborative initiatives have a role to play in connecting individual and collective action. Instead of investing in a single organization or project, they can encourage and guide participation efforts in collaboration with others. This is not a manipulative stance but leadership. It's a strategic marriage between financial and human resources conducted with ever-increasing transparency.

There are multiple planning frameworks that can be used to identify the strategic direction of a collaboration. In my consulting practice, I draw from a toolbox customized to fit the culture of the group as well as their stage of collaborative leadership development. The frameworks are important only insofar as they keep the group aligned. Solidifying relationships to one another and to the work remain primary.

With these strategies in place and our trust in one another growing, we are ready to act. Inherent in strategy design is an acceptance that our strategies are merely experiments, or threads to pull, on our most current understanding of an ever-changing issue. Next, we will put those experiments (and ourselves) to the test.

EXPERIMENTATION: TRIALS, FAILURES, AND RESILIENCE

The third stage is not only when we test our strategies but when we also test our engagement level. In the hero's journey, it's the point at which the hero must decide whether he has the courage and fortitude to stay the course. It's the same for the collective journey.

Experiments can feel like a curious exploration of what's possible or like a single shot at success. In the evolution of our leadership, we must choose to see it as the former. The road to a sustainable future is already fraught with challenges, and it will continue to be. If we are aware that we are on a long and sometimes perilous path toward something worthwhile, we are able to use the collaborative leadership practices to overcome resistance to what feels like impossible barriers. There will be victories too. And it's through this cycle of failure and victory that we learn more about who we are and that we are capable of weathering trials.

Experimentation is how we scale conservation at a more rapid pace. It's a constant calibration and recalibration to the effectiveness of our progress. The core of experimentation is not the experiments themselves but—once again—relationships. Therefore, we need a relational structure that guides our actions. We often refer to this structure as governance, but in the collaborative leadership model, there is more to consider than operational "rules." Traditional governance structures create rigidity that doesn't allow for failure. They often lead to a top-down attitude that doesn't engender shared responsibility for success.

One of the most powerful governance structures to create collective action comes from the Collective Impact Forum. They propose the following organizational structure to guide the experimentation process:[82]

- **An oversight group:** This is often what we think of as a board of directors or an executive committee. The members of this group are executive leaders from the participating organizations. They represent the diversity of stakeholders in the collaboration. This group meets regularly to oversee the progress of the entire initiative.
- **Working groups:** These groups form around the primary strategies. They are responsible for implementation. This includes identifying opportunities where partner organizations can integrate their individual work into the collaborative effort. Each working group operates separately from one another, though it's essential that they meet regularly to share data and stories about their progress, discuss challenges and opportunities, and maintain alignment to the shared vision, the issue, and each other.
- **The backbone organization:** This group serves as dedicated staff to the collaboration. They provide coordination for the shared work of the group, foster communication between the working and oversight groups, and measure progress toward goals. In the language of the collaborative leadership practices, they hold the container for the ongoing effort.

This decentralized structure requires structured approaches to communication. It's the only way to test the strategies' success. This happens through a cadence of regular meetings. Building

82   Fay Hanleybrown, John Kania, and Mark Kramer, "Channeling Change: Making Collective Impact Work," *Stanford Social Innovation Review*, January 26, 2012, https://ssir.org/articles/entry/channeling_change_making_collective_impact_work.

these meetings around the collaborative leadership practices helps us to examine our successes and failures. The practices help us return to the relational aspects of collaboration rather than solely focusing on data. They also remind us that we are not alone in our trials and failures. With this support, we feel emboldened to continue.

And yet, before we do, we must take a pause for evaluation.

THE PAUSE: ACCEPTING A NEW PATH

We set ourselves up for the pause long before we arrive at it. Somewhere between making the decision to act and the time we complete strategy design, we initiate the conversation about how we will collectively measure success. We need a way to understand whether our strategies are effective and whether we are making progress. If you've participated in any sort of strategic effort, the concept of measurement is not novel.

Developing shared measurements is more difficult in collaborations for all of the reasons we already know: diverse partners with different organizational missions come together to address multidimensional environmental issues in a synergistic way. In the face of this challenge, our habitual response is to adopt measures that individual partners already have in place. But these measures very rarely address system-level change. They are usually outcome-based, evaluating only a single aspect of the system.

Determining shared measurements for a collaboration takes as much energy and time as aligning under a common agenda. What's more, shared measurements look different at every stage of the collaboration. In the beginning, the evaluation will focus on what needs to happen. As the collaboration grows, questions will focus on how well it's working. It's only much later that any insight might be gained on the impact it made—especially given the long-term goals of systems-level change.

One approach is to define shared measurements for the strategies themselves. To do this well, collaborative leaders would do well to take a lesson from software developers who take the viewpoint of "failing fast." For them, goal attainment focuses on multiple cycles of testing and adaptation. In this approach, the data sets required for evaluation can happen at a smaller scale while keeping the ultimate goal in mind. This allows for strategies and tactics to be adjusted rapidly. What needs to be dropped? What needs to be added? What needs to be upgraded? This is the kind of nimbleness we need.

The pause is not just an evaluation of strategies and outcomes. It's also a time for considering how effectively we are working together. If I were to choose one measurement on which to evaluate the success of collaboration, it would be the strength of relationships among partners.[83] The reason for this is twofold: the relationships will outlive any formal initiative providing for future informal collaboration; relationships are synergistic.

Let's examine the importance of synergistic relationships. When we evaluate our goal, our strategies, or even our outcomes, it often becomes apparent that there is a barrier in our way to taking the next step. There is something or someone missing. New perspectives, knowledge, expertise, or experience

---

83 To my knowledge, there is not yet a formalized way to measure relationship. There is an opportunity for research on the impact on social networks. This would be extremely valuable data for collaborations to understand a different kind of progress. It would also provide funders with a tangible way to evaluate collaboration. Although we know that there is value in these partnerships, we haven't made visible how that operates.

might help us move forward. But where do those perspectives come from?

Enter the Connector.

In his book *The Tipping Point: How Little Things Can Make a Big Difference*, Malcolm Gladwell describes the Connector as someone who makes change happen through people. They can be the spark that ignites a movement because their life orientation is to establish quality relationships with a large number of people. When you present a problem to a Connector, they immediately begin to flip through their mental contact list to identify who they know that can provide help. Connectors are curious by nature and pursue experiences that have them engaged in multiple worlds with different types of people. They help us stop preaching to the choir and bring in a chorus of new voices.

Gladwell explains this as similar to the game Six Degrees of Kevin Bacon, in which you find the shortest path between an actor and Kevin Bacon. The idea being that you are never more than six degrees away. The game is a popularization of research into how social networks operate. Think of that. What if someone in your collaboration was only six degrees or less away from the answers you need? They probably are (or easily could be) if you knew the social map, the nodes of connection, and the hidden relationships that exist among your partners.

I've seen this arise over and over again in the work that I've done. Someone knows someone who knows someone. And they don't just *know* them, they have a trusting relationship. This relationship could be a game changer, but we don't know it exists. It could bring in someone with the expertise and resources that are needed at the exact right time. It might seem like a stroke of luck, but that's not the case. We are all Connectors in one way or another. But we often don't pause to evaluate those connections. Rather than waiting for them to emerge organically, we can be more deliberate. The end result is that we are able to draw in more partners, and we expand the reach of our collective action. If the relationships are strong, they live on, creating a synergistic bond that outlives formal actions, as I pointed to a moment ago.

Like the connections we make to and for each other, the pause shouldn't occur by happenstance. It should be built into the rhythm of the collaboration. There is no magic formula for how often the pause should occur—it largely depends on the types of strategies you are implementing. I recommend quarterly check-ins with my clients to create the "fail fast" momentum. The pause does require a deliberate assessment of results, but it also is the time when we continue our mastery of the collaborative leadership practices together.

While the collaborative leadership practices are not linear, the stages of our collective journey are. Each stage is a discrete stage that moves us forward until we eventually return to where we started and begin again.

There is one more stage through which we must pass. It's the stage where we return from the unknown world to the known, with the wisdom and fortitude built by accepting a new path. This final stage is our next evolution as collaborative leaders.

EMERGENCE: OUR LEADERSHIP EVOLUTION

Our collective journey results in collective action that is more than that of flashy heroics. We won't save the day, save the ecosystem, or save the planet in our first pass. But really, isn't that the beauty of this work? We don't have all the answers, nor are we expected to have them.

Success evolves over time—sometimes generations of time. We forget that, despite our understanding of and patience for the time that it takes for our environment to respond to new conditions. We want to see sweeping results of our efforts. The reality is that we might not. But what we *can* see is our leadership growth. We can even evaluate it through the lens of the adult development stages.

In the hero's journey, the protagonist returns to the known world with a gift to offer. The gift that we can offer is our growth. We bring the awareness and the tools back to others. We emerge holding ourselves accountable to being better leaders, setting the expectation that this is the new modus operandi for taking collective action on environmental issues.

Our collaborative efforts—whether directly as part of an ongoing structure or indirectly as the echoes of a more present, safe, diverse, healthy culture—last far beyond our tenure. The resilience we build through our fears and failures creates an immunity to change that the next generation can grow beyond. The villains might be overwhelming, but we've never been more powerful.

We're evolving. And our world will never be the same.

CONCLUSION

The big question is whether you are going to say a hearty yes to your adventure.

—JOSEPH CAMPBELL, AMERICAN PROFESSOR OF LITERATURE

We tend to look at evolution through a retrospective lens. We look back at how species have changed as a result of environmental factors, creative adaptations that helped them to thrive, and sometimes by a stroke of luck that put them in the right place at the right time. In the 1960s, a thirty-something-year-old ecologist named Roger Paine was a newly appointed assistant professor at the University of Washington. It was in the rocky tide pools of the Washington coastline that he made a profound discovery: there are certain species that play a crucial role in the survival of ecosystems.

He was studying the *Pisaster* starfish when he realized that it had a disproportional effect not only on the intertidal zones of the Pacific but on its shallow coastlines as well. Whether predator or prey, removing the starfish created a dramatic, detrimental impact. Upstream on the food chain, this impacted sea otters. Downstream on the food chain, this impacted mussel populations. One small, seemingly insignificant animal amplified our understanding of species evolution: *evolution happens in relationship*—to the environment, to other species, to one another.

A single species can be the essential link to maintaining the balance, diversity, and health of an entire community.

I wonder if Paine knew the ripple effect his work would create. Scientists pursued lines of research into species that were having similar effects in their ecosystems. The idea being that focused attention on a keystone species could ultimately impact whole landscapes—that we didn't have to look at the scope of the problem but the collective roles that each species had to play.

But there was one species that they missed in these investigations: humans.

Later in his life, Paine would raise this idea to the surface. He called humans the "hyperkeystone species." In his final paper, which published on the day that he died, he issued a call to action: "We are the influencer of influencers, the keystone species that disproportionately affects other keystone species, the Ur-stone that dictates the fate of every arch."[84]

If we look backward at our evolution, we can clearly see how we have impacted our planetary resources for as long as our species has been in existence. But what happens if we look forward? Can we intentionally change the role that we play as the "influencer of influencers?" Our innovations have often been for the benefit of our survival: from the harnessing of fire to the Industrial Revolution. But can we use that creative capacity to benefit not only ourselves but the entire web of life that supports us?

It might seem impossible, but we'll only know when we're all in.

THE FINAL CALL TO ADVENTURE

There are things that we can change about our outer world—our interactions with others, our role in society, the planet itself—that have an effect on who we are inside. But that inner world, what happens inside of us, has an arguably stronger impact. It drives our results and our future and is the source of leadership that is generative and whole. The practices of collaborative leadership begin within before expanding outward toward the collective. That's where our creative power is found.

A new way to look at collaborative leadership is as provision for

---

84   Ed Yong, "Humans: The Hyperkeystone Species," *The Atlantic*, June 21, 2016, https://www. theatlantic.com/science/archive/2016/06/humans-the-hyperkeystone-species/487985/.

a future generation. It's something that we're not only building for the world as it is now but as a legacy for the world that our children and grandchildren will inherit.

Most of the changes that we set in motion will affect the world in ways that we won't get to see. Performance goals won't align with this kind of work—we have to set developmental goals. We have to find new ways of measuring, new ways of being, new ways of finding value in our work.

We are changing the leadership ecosystem so that all of the natural world—including the people who depend on it—can thrive.

Some of us will set out on bigger journeys than others. Some of us will find each other as our individual purpose blends with new collaborations down the line. In those moments—when we've decided to set out on a learning journey together to combine our experiences and meaning and efforts until we spark some kind of change—we become the springboard for a leadership evolution.

You see, we are not the starfish of Paine's research. We have creative capacity that carries us far beyond sustenance and into acceleration. We can be intentional about our relationships to one another, to ourselves, and to the way we operate in the world. The only catch is that we can't do it alone.

There's vulnerability in asking for help. There's beauty in giving up on ego and surrendering to the path ahead. Find each other. Find a guide. Practice. Trust that even your guides are practicing—and that none of us will get it exactly right. Hold space for yourself and allow others to hold space for you. Come back to that moment where your childlike senses caught a glimpse of the beauty of this planet for the very first time, and the call to adventure started in earnest.

You're doing something immensely challenging here. Don't do it alone.

ABOUT THE AUTHOR

LAURA CALANDRELLA is a leadership strategist and consultant. She has spent the past two decades working with organizations from across the environmental community to design collaborative approaches to our most pressing issues. Her career began as a conservation biologist and international development practitioner. These experiences gave Laura firsthand knowledge of the power of collaboration but also the difficulties that arise when diverse perspectives align under a shared vision for change. Now she guides the growth of sustainability and conservation partnerships by teaching the practices of collaborative leadership. Her work strengthens relationships, delivers more holistic and creative solutions, and allows her clients to achieve impactful results at increasingly larger scales.

Made in the USA
Coppell, TX
19 January 2021